SOURCING AND SELECTING TEXTILES FOR FASHION

Erin Cadigan

Fairchild Books
An imprint of Bloomsbury Publishing Plc

50 Bedford Square	1385 Broadway
London	New York
WC1B 3DP	NY 10018
UK	USA

www.bloomsbury.com

Bloomsbury is a registered trademark of
Bloomsbury Publishing Plc

First published 2014
© Bloomsbury Publishing Plc, 2014

British Library Cataloguing-in-Publication Data
A catalogue record for this book is available from the
British Library.

ISBN: PB: 978-2-940496-10-5
ePDF: 978-2-940447-67-1

Library of Congress Cataloging-in-Publication Data
Cadigan, Erin.
Sourcing and selecting textiles for fashion / Erin Cadigan.
pages cm
ISBN 978-2-940496-10-5 (pbk.) -- ISBN 978-2-940447-67-1 ()
1. Dressmaking materials. 2. Textile fabrics. I. Title.
TT557.C33 2013
646.4--dc23
2013020875

Design by Andrew Howard
Printed and bound in China

1 Backstage at Duro Olowu, Autumn/Winter 2012. Duro Olowu designs most of his fabrics and prints himself but also incorporates vintage textiles.

CHAPTER FIVE / 132
SOURCING YOUR FABRIC

CHAPTER SIX / 154
TEXTILES AND
THE COLLECTION

SOURCING INTERVIEWS / 174

APPENDIX / 198

INTRODUCTION

Sourcing and Selecting Textiles for Fashion advances the understanding of the key relationships between textile selection, textile design and fashion design. Textiles and fashion are often viewed as two related yet separate industries. Today, designers of every level have the opportunity, through the rise of technology and access to global sourcing, to conceptualize the design of not only the end fashion product but also the textiles involved. Traditionally textbooks offer a deep perspective on one, while offering a brief look at the other. *Sourcing and Selecting Textiles for Fashion* offers a fresh look at how both influence and support each other.

The aim of this book is to present the student with the knowledge necessary to design a creative and aesthetically pleasing fashion collection through correct textile choice. In order to realize their vision, a designer must understand the relationship a textile's design, function and inherent properties play in the process from conceptual two-dimensional design to a three-dimensional garment. While style and fashions are constantly in flux, the building blocks of good design remain static. Advances in technology continue to add innovative new properties and design capabilities to textile, yet the core relationship of form and pattern to the human body remains the same. This book offers the firm foundational knowledge of textile and design needed in the fantastical and flighty world of fashion.

Sourcing and Selecting Textiles for Fashion is written both for the fashion student who desires a thorough knowledge of how textile selection influences design and for the textile designer who hopes to have a better understanding of how their work may influence the end product. The alliance between textile and fashion is broad and ever changing. This book highlights the important influential connections between the two, offering a manageable guide to current methods of design in both fields.

The format of the book follows the informational sequence a design professional would use to conceptualize a fashion collection. By starting with a historical and industrial overview of the connection between textile design and its impact on fashion, the reader learns to look outside themselves at the influence of politics, trade, technology, culture and environmental concern on production, availability and style. Through the comprehension of fashion textile as a historical, cultural and socio art form the student starts to assemble their personal stylistic and ethical approach to fashion design.

The text next examines the fibres used to create textiles, the various methods of production and the many resulting types of materials available in the current market. This offers a broad look at man-made and natural fibres and the many ways they may be woven, knit or manipulated to create the large range of fabrics available today. Examining the finishing and dyeing process, the book instructs on the environmental and social impact of textile production.

The designer goes on to learn of the many ways a basic textile may be enhanced through contemporary surface design methods. Both industrial and DIY perspectives are offered on a range of decorative applications including dyeing, printing, pattern, embellishment and fabric manipulation. A discussion on the planning and placement of surface design is started.

Armed with this vital knowledge, the student uses the second half of the text to work through the steps of conceptualizing, sourcing and designing textiles for the development of a fashion line or collection. The book covers how to define your target market, choose an inspiration, consider the roles of trend and colour, visualize thematic silhouette and consider whether or not to add surface design. Within this discussion the text makes the student aware of the cost vs. value each decision adds to the final product.

The next section teaches the student about the options for sourcing the perfect fabric for their line. It presents practical information about the supply chain and defines the retail source options for a designer at any level in their fashion career. Comprehensive explanations are given on fabric properties and characteristics with a list of the common textiles where each can be found. This section includes instruction on how to create, design and produce custom textiles.

The final chapter focuses on teaching the student how to apply all these aspects of textile selection into a cohesive and saleable fashion collection. It covers the many outside influences on fabric and design choice such as availability, cost and ethical concerns and how to marry those with inspiration and creative intention. The specialized construction considerations of certain fabrics are also looked at. The book considers the applied methods of two-dimensional conceptualization, both hand rendering and CAD and touches on three-dimensional conceptualization through drape. Lastly it informs the student how to use these informational techniques to edit and refine the collection prior to sampling.

An additional supplemental section has been added to the text spotlighting designers at different stages of their careers and levels of market. The focus of these interviews is to share the varied ways professionals source, create and conceptualize the textile selections for their lines.

The content of *Sourcing and Selecting Textiles for Fashion* is presented in an accessible fashion. For the novice, the information is best processed in the order it is presented. This way the student forms a systematic method for conceptualizing the interrelated roles of textile on fashion and fashion on textile. Once the material is familiar to the designer, the book becomes a handy reference for specific knowledge. It is intended that the user will return to it again and again to help define the direction in which to take their design work.

In addition the text is illuminated with pictorial examples of both student and professional design work. Throughout the book, quotes, informational highlights, charts, designer spotlights and interviews keep the reader's interest and add to their sense of connection with the fashion industry. Further self-motivated discovery is encouraged through the appendices, which offer common industry terminology, textile sourcing resources and links to related designers, websites and publications.

CHAPTER ONE

The Role of Textiles in Fashion

To know fashion one must also know textiles. Without an intimate understanding of his materials, no artist will be able to produce his best work. Fashion design is no different. Good design can start with the right bolt of cloth. But how does a designer know what the right fabric choice is?

By forming a database of textile knowledge you will be well equipped to make educated decisions that will enhance your design capabilities and help produce your best work. It is important that you have a working knowledge of the long history and interplay of fashion and textiles. Consideration should be given to where the fabric comes from and how its print or pattern impacts the viewer. In terms of silhouette and construction a designer must understand the functional capabilities of the cloth. Does it have body? Will it drape? Does it need to fulfill certain aesthetic or protective functions? Will the resulting product require special (perhaps expensive) finishing methods? As you learn more about inspiration, function, properties of fabric, colour and texture, you will grow as an artist.

Designers today are also faced with complex ethical considerations. The world has woken up to the impact of the fashion industry on our environment and the health of factory workers. Globalization has pushed many traditional textile handicrafts to the point of extinction. Luckily there are many different paths within textile and fashion development that a designer can choose to make a positive impact in small or large ways. Every conscious step is a step in the right direction.

Fashion is not something that exists in dresses only. Fashion is in the sky, in the street, fashion has to do with ideas, the way we live, what is happening.
Coco Chanel

**SOURCING AND SELECTING
TEXTILES FOR FASHION**

CHAPTER ONE: THE ROLE OF TEXTILES IN FASHION
CHAPTER TWO: MATERIALS
CHAPTER THREE: SURFACE DESIGN
CHAPTER FOUR: CONCEPTUALIZING THE COLLECTION
CHAPTER FIVE: SOURCING YOUR FABRIC
CHAPTER SIX: TEXTILES AND THE COLLECTION
SOURCING INTERVIEWS
APPENDIX

12

The farther backward you can look, the farther forward you can see.
Winston Churchill

TEXTILE CULTURE

The history of textile culture is a glimpse at the history of world culture. Every global society that has ever existed has encased their bodies in a textile of some sort. Within primitive societies apparel began as a matter of protection from the elements. Yet even in man's first tribal clans, body coverings quickly took on decoration and meaning. As society became more cultured, civilized and aware, the decorative symbolism and styles of what was covering our bodies advanced hand-in-hand with world culture. Textiles started to tell stories about a wearer's region of origin, social status, trade and religious role.

As a designer it is important to understand the long interwoven history of textile, fashion and social structure. The influence of the textile and fashion industries has impacted politics, lifestyles, laws and technological advancements throughout human history. Likewise, each of these social structures has affected the clothing styles and fashion fads of each passing era. In order to look forward with innovative vision a designer must understand how current social mores impact their design choices, as well as how textile and fashion history can continue to influence and inspire collections today.

Primitive culture

The textile and clothing development of primitive cultures was one of location and function. Tied closely to his environment, tribal man sourced locally for materials with which to clothe himself. Archaeological and anthropological discoveries have shown varied and creative sourcing of local animals, minerals and plants used in textiles worldwide. The leathers, furs, woven fabrics, natural dyes and decorative elements of these ancient societies remain an important inspirational resource for modern design. As today's designers become more aware of sustainability issues and the loss of traditional construction techniques, there has been a strong movement towards finding, preserving and acknowledging the importance of primitive design and methodology.

1 The techniques of draping and gathering textiles to fit the human form were used early on in women's fashion.

13

TEXTILE CULTURE
EVOLUTION OF TEXTILE DESIGN
GLOBAL TEXTILE PRODUCTION
A CALL FOR SUSTAINABILITY
CERTIFICATIONS AND LABELLING
DESIGNER SPOTLIGHT – MISSONI

PRIMITIVE TEXTILE HISTORY

On the African continent primitive tribes wove animal hair, along with local plants and tree fibres into their textiles. Indigo was their most important dye (Spring, 1993).

A primitive iceman, nicknamed Otzi, was discovered in 1991 by hikers in the Tyrolean Alps. The glacier had helped preserve the most comprehensive outfit of Neolithic European man including patchworked fur hat, leggings and sleeveless tunic; cowhide loincloth, grass-lined shoes and a full knee-length cape made of woven grasses for protection (Casanovas, 2001).

The world's oldest fragment of woven cloth was discovered in a Turkish village on the Tigris river. Carbon dated to 7,000 BC, it is a type of linen made from flax-like fibre (Wilford, 1993).

Native tribes of North America mainly wore clothes made of animal skins elaborately decorated with beading and embroidery made of quills, animal tails, feathers and shells.

In Asia the Chinese have been producing silk fabrics for 5,000 years. However the earliest textile fragment found in Asia is cloth made from kohemp, a fibre produced from the kudzu vine, which is over 5,700 years old (Cultural China, no date).

The ancient world

As insular, land-based tribal societies moved to the sprawling cultural centres of Egypt, Greece and Rome, textile and fashion moved away from animal skins. Loom-woven textiles became prevalent. **Draping** sheets of fabric to create silhouette and decorative form flourished during this time. Highly stylized metal clasps, belts and pins often inlaid with precious stones and enamel helped fasten these complex fashions to the body. The influence of this historic period's stylized draping and pleating can often be seen in modern fashion collections.

The most common textiles in use throughout the ancient world were **linen** and, as the centuries advanced, **wool**. Linen was created from long staple fibres stripped from stalk plants like flax while wool was made from the hair of sheep or goats. The ancients used various methods of fashionable surface decoration on their garments including bleaching, dyeing, braiding, fringe, sequins, beading and embroidery.

Silk Road

Textile and fashion have been important twin economies as far back as recorded history. Textile development can be equated to cultural cuisine development. Due to localized ingredients of fibres, dyestuff, tastes and methodology, every part of the world had its own distinct flavour. As global trade routes opened up, fabric became a staple offering. Textiles travelled well, were non-perishable and everyone needed to clothe him or herself. As societies became more mobile and therefore globally aware, the lust for exotic products grew. Textiles from far-away lands for use in home or fashion became a status symbol and a profitable business.

The Silk Road was an overland trade route that linked East, South and West Asia with Europe, the Middle East and Africa. In addition to the land-based route there was also a Marine Silk Road that linked China by sea with Vietnam, Thailand and eventually India. The journey of silk from China to Europe could take over a year making the price of this textile equal to gold. China was the world's dominant silk producer well into the early twentieth century (<www.yuanhousilk.com>).

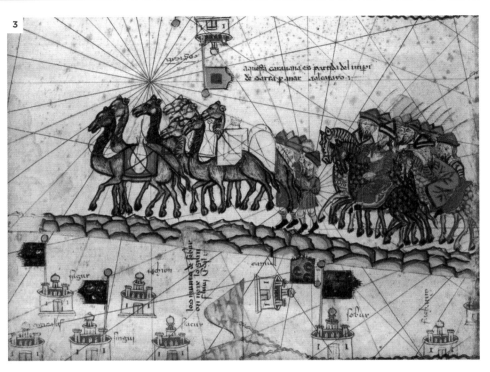

2 The pleated, draped and decorated fashions of ancient Egypt, as depicted in murals of Queen Nefertari at her tomb.

3 Silk Road merchants on the ancient trade route through Asia. From an illuminated 1375 Mallorcan manuscript.

Medieval times, 400–1400

Society expanded north and Europe became a central figure in the modern world. In the 800s, Emperor Charlemagne ruled much of modern France, Germany and Italy. His sumptuary laws regulating the price of clothing and the vastness of his empire helped develop the social system of fashion. A new type of socio-political structure called feudalism emerged, creating a tiered scheme of wealth and prosperity. This system allowed for a middle class of merchants and tradesmen to prosper. Trade merchants brought in exotic fabrics and weavers and tailors, having the time to focus on their craft, expanded the understanding of fit, form and design. Clothing for the rich became ornate and complex. Women wore dresses with elaborately silhouetted sleeves, fitted bodices and full skirts made of rich brocade silk, satins and finely woven cottons in bright colours. Surface design of embroidery, beading, lace and contrasting appliqué was common. Men wore decorative tunics and fitted leggings. The middle classes wore similar looks in slimmed down silhouettes made of lower quality linens, cottons and wool. The serfs, both men and women, wore loose woollen robes and dresses fitted with lacing and belts. All levels of society wore a frequently washed undergarment called a **chemise**. The chemise was a simple woven tunic with set-in sleeves that drew into gathers at the wrist and neck.

TEXTILE CULTURE
EVOLUTION OF TEXTILE DESIGN
GLOBAL TEXTILE PRODUCTION
A CALL FOR SUSTAINABILITY
CERTIFICATIONS AND LABELLING
DESIGNER SPOTLIGHT – MISSONI

1500s

In the sixteenth century, Lyon, France and some northern Italian cities became known for their weaving of raw imported silk. This century also saw a move of production to the New World. Mexico's weavers and textile artisans produced satins, damasks, velvets and other fabrics using raw Chinese silk fibres (De la Fuente, 2008, pp. 27–8).

Fashion became an elaborate status symbol. Padding of both men and women's clothing to create extreme silhouettes was popularized. Laws were passed to keep citizens dressing according to their station and people dressing above their lot in life could be arrested and fined. A new fashion of 'slashing', literally slicing the fabric of an outer garment to reveal brightly coloured insets of contrasting fabric or elaborately decorated undergarments, became popular. This fad is a prime example of the **'trickle-down effect'** in which fashion moves from the upper strata of society, in this case the aristocracy and military, to the general population becoming a universal fashion movement.

1600s

By the seventeenth century, Europe's woven and embroidered textiles were extravagantly patterned. Printed fabrics in similar motifs were seen as cheap knock offs regulated to the lower classes. As trade with India grew during the 1600s, gorgeous, hand-painted textiles featuring ornate floral designs flooded the markets of Europe. These **chintz** fabrics were not easy for European textile houses to replicate and became the first high-end printed fabrics. In order to keep up with production demands from the European market, Indian designers produced less unique hand-painted fabrics and more repeat **block prints**. Textile artists would carve the ornate elements into wooden blocks, dipping them into a **mordant dye** substance and hand print the designs across the fabric.

Boning, the use of wood, ivory or bone strips sewn into the fabric to create structure and form, became popular for women's corsets and eliminated the need for lacing. Embroidered petticoats started to peek out from under women's skirts and bodices exposed the shoulder. The 1600s also introduced a fashion phenomenon in accessories for men and women, the heeled shoe or boot.

4

CHAPTER ONE: THE ROLE OF TEXTILES IN FASHION

17

TEXTILE CULTURE
EVOLUTION OF TEXTILE DESIGN
GLOBAL TEXTILE PRODUCTION
A CALL FOR SUSTAINABILITY
CERTIFICATIONS AND LABELLING
DESIGNER SPOTLIGHT – MISSONI

THE IMPACT OF CALICO

A perfect example of the symbiotic influence of textile, fashion and society is calico cloth. Its history impacts trade, fashion, law, politics, industrial growth and invention.

Calico refers to both the thin, woven cotton cloth itself and also the repeat patterns applied to it, often floral or nature based. This fabric originated in Asia, mainly India and Turkey, and was imported to Europe along the Silk Road. It became so popular for home and apparel that it threatened the sub-par European printed fabrics, causing many nations to ban the wearing or production of all printed textiles.

Eventually, copper plate printing was invented to improve Europe's printed offerings. As the desire for fine cotton calico grew in Europe, this fashion fad directly impacted trade with the Americas and the growth of a newly burgeoning cotton industry there.

In Europe, new methods of printing fabrics and the creation of permanent dyestuff continued to be developed in a race to replace the higher quality Asian calicoes.

Irish calico artist William Kilburn's multicolour calico prints became so popular he was forced to apply for a bill to protect his intellectual rights. The bill, passed in May 1787 'An Act for the Encouragement of the Arts of designing & printing Linens, Cottons, Calicoes & Muslins by vesting the Properties thereof in the Designers, Printers, Proprietors for a limited Time', is one of the first artistic copyright laws.

1700s

In 1752, an Irish textile designer named Francis Dixon developed **copper plate printing**. The plate engraving process allowed for highly detailed pictorial designs to be printed in one colour on a light hued fabric. The prints illustrated scenes of nineteenth-century life, mythology, hunting scenes, pastoral scenes and floral arrangements. The resulting textile, **toile** was instrumental in the eradication of the printed textile ban. Today, these patterns are commonly called 'toile de Jouy' due to the overwhelming popularity of the prints from one factory in the French town of Jouy-en-Josas. Embroidery continued to be an important surface design element with royal houses and religious orders often employing in-house artisans.

The free thinking society of the 1700s **Rococo** period resulted in fashions becoming less rigid structurally. Gone were the dark colours and heavy fabrics of the **Baroque** 1600s. Dresses made of pretty pastel coloured fabrics closely followed the human form. Towards the end of the 1700s, fashions looked back to the simplicity of ancient Greek and Roman drapery. Dresses lost all structured corseting and were often made of gauzy cotton **muslin**.

1800s and the Industrial Revolution

During the 1800s mechanized manufacturing advancements in the textile industries led the world into a major industrial turning point. The first textile factory opened in England employing the **Spinning Jenny**, a machine able to do the work of eight hand spinners. With the continued popularity of cotton fabrics, the United States became a major player in textiles, supplying Europe with much of its raw cotton fibre. Textile mills opened across America's eastern seaboard. With the financial support of Emperor Napoleon Bonaparte, silk production remained strong in France due to patriotic concern for its textile industry.

Other major technological inventions included the steam engine powered loom, the jacquard loom, the roller printer, power pattern looms, multicolour roller printing and mechanized lace production. In addition to mechanical advancements, chemistry started to be applied to fashion, specifically in the dye industry. In 1856, William Henry Perkins accidentally created the world's first organic chemical dye and within a decade, an industry was launched producing synthetic dyes of every colour. All this came at a human cost. Massive factories replaced artisan shops. Skilled tradesmen lost their status and often their livelihood. Unskilled factory workers were saddled with long hours, unsafe conditions and very low wages. Industrial waste became a by-product of the fashion industry.

4 Late 1700s calico print by Irish artist William Kilburn (1745–1818).

**SOURCING AND SELECTING
TEXTILES FOR FASHION**

CHAPTER ONE: THE ROLE OF TEXTILES IN FASHION
CHAPTER TWO: MATERIALS
CHAPTER THREE: SURFACE DESIGN
CHAPTER FOUR: CONCEPTUALIZING THE COLLECTION
CHAPTER FIVE: SOURCING YOUR FABRIC
CHAPTER SIX: TEXTILES AND THE COLLECTION
SOURCING INTERVIEWS
APPENDIX

18

5 Evening dress by Charles Fredrick Worth, noted as the first fashion designer (1826–95).

6 By 1900 the textile mill was a well-established feature of urban America, producing goods in response to the ever-increasing consumer demand.

1850s–1900

In England, the mid-century **Arts and Crafts Movement** was a backlash against the technological loss of artisanal arts. Morris & Co, led by William Morris, focused on bringing back hand block and discharge printing incorporating the use of naturally derived textile dyes rather than the newly manufactured industrial dyes. The arts and crafts motifs eventually developed into the **art nouveau** style, which focused on flowing and curved lines coupled with natural forms (Watt, 2000).

The 1800s gave the world its first fashion design house. Textile expert and dressmaker Charles Frederick Worth founded the House of Worth in 1858. As was traditional, House of Worth created couture pieces for their clientele. Unlike many dressmakers of the time they also showcased ready-made fashions on live models. Worth is credited with being the first designer to employ fashion sketching to work out his elaborate designs for sale to clients prior to manufacturing the garment.

1900–1920s

The dawn of the twentieth century brought in a new age of invention, global connectedness and style. Building on the industrial advances of the previous century, the world started to change at a pace never before seen. In the textile industry, the progressive knowledge of chemistry was applied to the creation of man-made fibres resulting in **synthetic fabrics**. During the first few decades of the 1900s, the synthetic fabrics **acetate**, **viscose** and **rayon** were produced using a cellulose compound originating from wood. Chemistry was also applied to further the advance of industrial dyes resulting in **vat dyes**, a category of dyes with extremely good fastness to light and washing.

With the opening of factories and the industrialization of the textile industry, women moved into the workforce in new numbers. Fashion became a commercial enterprise accessible to the masses. Fashion magazines with exquisite illustrations of current textile and fashion trends came into vogue. Women's fashion silhouette became rectangular with an empire waist. Designers such as Paul Poiret, Mariano Fortuny and Madeleine Vionnet brought in major influences from ancient Greece and the Orient, finding new ways to apply **drape, vertical pleats, over dyeing** and **bias cut** fabric to women's fashions.

19

TEXTILE CULTURE
EVOLUTION OF TEXTILE DESIGN
GLOBAL TEXTILE PRODUCTION
A CALL FOR SUSTAINABILITY
CERTIFICATIONS AND LABELLING
DESIGNER SPOTLIGHT – MISSONI

Sportswear has more to do than anything else with the evolution of the modern mode.
Vogue magazine 1926

1925–1940s

Following on the heels of World War I came the 1920s. The first decade of modern relaxed society influenced fashions for both men and women. By 1925, the roaring twenties saw women in short skirts and trousers, and men in casual athletic wear. The flatbed purl-knitting machine invented earlier in the century sped production of knit textiles and designer Coco Chanel, impacted fashion for generations to come with the simple lines of her jersey knit suits. The trend of simplicity carried forward into the 1930s. The world was just emerging from the Great Depression and practicality and restraint reigned even in the world of fashion. Daywear became a major focus of designers, notable for simple cuts, separates (rather than dresses) and cheaper, sturdier fabrics. The military influence of both World War I and World War II impacted men and women's fashions with padded shoulders, tailored cuts and pockets. The world's first truly synthetic textile, **nylon**, made its debut in hosiery and the zipper became the apparel closure of choice.

1945–1950s

As World War II came to a close the world was tired of the austerity measures of the depression and wartime. Christian Dior's New Look took the trend away from the slim structured silhouettes of the earlier decades. It reintroduced a soft femininity and was characterized by form-fitting tops and excessively full skirts. The manufacturing plants of wartime focused on technologies for home and the textile industries turned out many new synthetic fabrics and easy-care finishes for clothing. **Nylon** sheers, easy to wash **polyester, spandex** stretch and silky **rayon** helped designers create new styles. Mass manufacturing brought fast, inexpensive fashion.

During the 1950s, technology and mechanized appliances moved into people's homes freeing up unheard of amounts of leisure time. Rock and roll, television and the teenager created a new focus on youth culture. The combination of inexpensive easily washed fabrics, casual living and the new youth market brought about the biggest changes in women's styles the world had ever seen. Casual and dress trousers in fitted stretch fabrics, strapless tops worn for day held up by new synthetic undergarments and full circle skirts worn with easy to clean white and pastel twin sets were popular styles. Two of fashion's most enduring **trickle-up trends** started in menswear and crossed over to womenswear. Based on blue-collar work apparel and immortalized by actor Marlon Brando in *The Wild Ones*, the T-shirt and the denim jean became American fashion staples.

7 During World War II women's fashion silhouette became tailored to the body with a raised hemline in an effort to use less fabric.

SOURCING AND SELECTING
TEXTILES FOR FASHION

CHAPTER ONE: THE ROLE OF TEXTILES IN FASHION
CHAPTER TWO: MATERIALS
CHAPTER THREE: SURFACE DESIGN
CHAPTER FOUR: CONCEPTUALIZING THE COLLECTION
CHAPTER FIVE: SOURCING YOUR FABRIC
CHAPTER SIX: TEXTILES AND THE COLLECTION
SOURCING INTERVIEWS
APPENDIX

20

8

8 Swinging sixties icon, English actress and activist Jane Birkin in a romantic 1960s look by designer Ossie Clark.

1960s

At the dawning of the 1960s, America and much of the world was focused on the arms race and getting to the moon. In fashion and textiles, this translated to perceived futuristic silhouettes, prints and materials. Textile designs inspired by abstract art focused on **op art** illusions and bold black and white graphics. Fashion designers Emanuel Ungaro and Paco Rabanne created very short, modular looking designs out of non-fabric materials like paper, wood, metal and plastic. The industrial textile, **vinyl**, found its way into fashion styles and **Kevlar**, the world's first flame- and abrasion-resistant engineered textile was introduced. The end of the decade saw America embroiled in the unpopular Vietnam War and a fight for equal rights for minorities and women. Silhouettes turned romantic and nostalgic. Psychedelic mind expansion and an obsession with Eastern religious philosophy affected everything from prints and silhouettes to fabric selection.

1970s

Economic reforms in the 1970s encouraged textile manufacturers out of Europe and the United States into less developed countries like China and Taiwan. With advanced manipulation of the synthetic fibre, **polyester** was made to cheaply mimic many different natural textile properties, increasing designers' use of synthetics for fashion. At the same time a new movement of concern for the environment and the loss of traditional arts saw the first stirrings of **sustainability** and a return to **handicraft** in fashion. Designer Donna Karan wowed women with her easy-to-fit wrap dress, Vivienne Westwood introduced the fashion world to the extreme styling of punk. Dominant American and European designers moved over to share the stage with minimalist Japanese designers like Rei Kawakubo and Yohji Yamamoto.

1980s

In the 1980s, the fashion silhouette was a designer's playground; no one look dominated the runways. Structured, unstructured, underwear as outerwear, excessively padded shoulders, body conscious stretch fits, bubble skirts, **mini-crinis,** prairie skirts; street wear, club wear, rap influences, glam influences, Laura Ashley's Old World romantic florals, Stephen Sprouse's graffiti prints, the androgyny of rock icons Boy George and Annie Lennox; the 1980s wore it all. Extreme individuality ruled this decade, yet the fashion label as status symbol permeated almost all market levels from high end Gucci suits and Louis Vuitton handbags to the hold sportswear giants Adidas and Puma had over the streets.

21

TEXTILE CULTURE
EVOLUTION OF TEXTILE DESIGN
GLOBAL TEXTILE PRODUCTION
A CALL FOR SUSTAINABILITY
CERTIFICATIONS AND LABELLING
DESIGNER SPOTLIGHT – MISSONI

9

9 Party-goer Agyness Deyn at the Louis Vuitton Tribute to Stephen Sprouse.

1990s

After the excessive fashions of the 1980s, the next decade quietened down. The world economies took a nosedive and the blue-collar, rock music influence of **grunge** spread out of America's Pacific Northwest. Characterized by plaid flannel shirts, thrift shop tees, ripped jeans and work boots, designer Marc Jacobs turned the grunge look into a fully fledged fashion movement with his notorious Spring 93 collection for Perry Ellis. Not everyone was enamoured by the layered, poverty look; many designers strove to capture a serious, pared down minimalism. Smart simple silhouettes, neutral colours and high quality, high tech textiles characterized this utilitarian look, made popular by designers Helmut Lang, Miuccia Prada and Jil Sander. In the youth market, crazy rave club wear, dark goth looks and extreme fashions of the 1960s and 70s reigned. Sustainability started to gain momentum with recycling, anti-fur and ecologically friendly fibres.

2000–present

Fashion at the turn of the twenty-first century has had a hard time defining itself. The instant information and shopping accessibility of the Internet, world domination of homogenized big box stores, globalization of trade, and decline of traditional fashion production mills in the migration towards cheaper labour have all taken their toll on the way the world understands fashion. There has been a rise of individualized anti-fashion as people have been overwhelmed with instantaneous fads and mountains of cheaply made, fast-fashion items. From these seemingly negative trends have arisen some interesting and positive fashion paths. Thanks to the Internet for the first time young and niche designers have really been able to survive and grow their businesses in an economically feasible way. As a result of the popularity of the inexpensive fashion item, well-known designers have taken a look at the reach of their luxury products. This self-reflection of economic infeasibility has led to **high-low fashion collaborations** such as Versace for H&M, Mary Katrantzou for Topshop and Missoni for Target, allowing the general population to own designer pieces for a fraction of the cost. The positive aspect of globalization is the rise of micro-economies built on traditional textile handicrafts and the influence of fresh designers from places like Africa, Argentina and India. The hyper production schedule of all this fast fashion has turned the world's conscious focus towards the environmental and human toll of the textile and fashion industries. Sustainability and social reform in these industries have been a hallmark of twenty-first century design.

SOURCING AND SELECTING
TEXTILES FOR FASHION

CHAPTER ONE: THE ROLE OF TEXTILES IN FASHION
CHAPTER TWO: MATERIALS
CHAPTER THREE: SURFACE DESIGN
CHAPTER FOUR: CONCEPTUALIZING THE COLLECTION
CHAPTER FIVE: SOURCING YOUR FABRIC
CHAPTER SIX: TEXTILES AND THE COLLECTION
SOURCING INTERVIEWS
APPENDIX

22

TRADITIONAL TEXTILES OF AFRICA AND ASIA

Adinkra (Africa, Ghana)
Stamped and embroidered cloth of dyed woven cotton.

Adire (Africa, Nigeria)
Over dyed fabric created by tiedye, or dye resist from stitched raffia or cassava paste; often indigo coloured.

Damask (Arabia)
Often one colour, reversible fabric utilizing long floats of both warp and weft to create patterns that reflect light differently according to the position of the fabric.

Kente (Africa, Ghana)
Woven patterned cloth using red, yellow, green, blue, gold, white and black to represent beliefs and customs and weave patterns to represent religion, politics, financial position or a special occasion.

Mud (Africa, Mali)
Sewn strips of hand spun and woven cotton, under-dyed with a yellow bark dye and painted with fermented mud. Typically shades of white, yellow, purple, beige, rich brown and rust.

Shibori (Asia, Japan)
Silk, cotton or hemp woven fabric tie dyed by binding, folding, stitching, capping, twisting or compressing the fabric, traditionally white cloth dyed with madder (red), indigo (blue) or purple root.

EVOLUTION OF TEXTILE DESIGN

Two of the most important aspects of textile design are print and materials. Many common textile designs in use today are inspired by or taken directly from traditional textiles and fabrics. Designers have a long history of mining the past for inspiration. As we noted in the previous section, much of traditional Western textile and fashion influence has come from European, Asian and American cultures. In today's global society it has become essential to expand one's knowledge to recognize all world history as having value and acknowledge multicultural contributions to world style. It is imperative when looking to another's culture for inspiration that a designer does so in a respectful manner.

Africa

African textiles were woven from cotton, animal hair, silk, raffia, bark and jute. Designs were used as a way to communicate origin, spirituality and folklore, and to commemorate events and denote status. Imagery was highly stylized pictographs or symbolic repeat patterns. Patterns were woven into the fabric by spot dyeing the warp yarns or weaving thicker strips of coloured fabrics in both weft and warp. Pictorial prints were stamped, embroidered, appliquéd and hand painted. Colours were earth tones: browns and greens from soil and plants, reds from oxidized metals, and indigo for rich blues and purples.

Asia

Asia is known for its advanced and early production of silk textiles, worn primarily by the aristocracy and traded as an export. Other plant-based fibres such as hemp, ramie (a common garden weed) and cotton were worn by the general population. Damask and brocade patterned fabrics originated in China. Other methods of decoration include delicate and detailed embroidery, silkscreen printing, block printing, resist, shibori dye techniques and hand painting. Imagery was stylized, realistic pictures of flora, fauna, landscapes and life. Geometric and mandala shapes symbolized beliefs in politics, family and spirituality.

23

TEXTILE CULTURE
EVOLUTION OF TEXTILE DESIGN
GLOBAL TEXTILE PRODUCTION
A CALL FOR SUSTAINABILITY
CERTIFICATIONS AND LABELLING
DESIGNER SPOTLIGHT – MISSONI

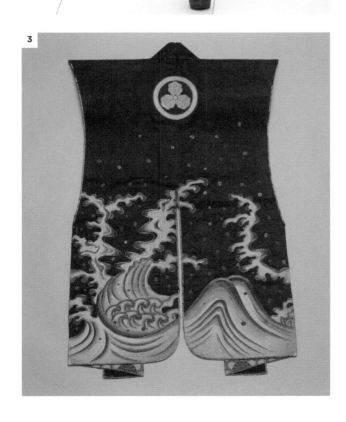

1 African influence: Machine-printed African patterns based on traditional kente cloth walk the runway at Burberry Prorsum autumn 2012.

2 Traditional African dress: Symbolic of the leopard, masquerade tunic, late nineteenth–early twentieth century. Kingdom of Bamilike, Cameroon Grassfields. Plant fibre, human hair.

3 Traditional Asian dress: Samurai waves surcoat (jimbaori), Edo period (1615–1868), Japan. Silk, felt, metallic thread, lacquered wood.

4 Asian influence: Christian Dior spring 2007 couture collection.

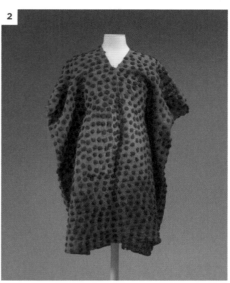

SOURCING AND SELECTING
TEXTILES FOR FASHION

CHAPTER ONE: THE ROLE OF TEXTILES IN FASHION
CHAPTER TWO: MATERIALS
CHAPTER THREE: SURFACE DESIGN
CHAPTER FOUR: CONCEPTUALIZING THE COLLECTION
CHAPTER FIVE: SOURCING YOUR FABRIC
CHAPTER SIX: TEXTILES AND THE COLLECTION
SOURCING INTERVIEWS
APPENDIX

24

TRADITIONAL TEXTILES OF INDIA AND EUROPE

Chintz (India) Glazed woven cotton fabric with a stained or painted calico pattern.

Fair Isle (North-West Europe) Knit patterned fabric, knitted in the round from no more than five colours. Knitting with a select colour creates the pattern while unused colours float across fabric backing until knitted into pattern.

Linen (Middle East, Eastern Europe) Woven fabric created from long staple fibres of the flax plant. Most likely the oldest textile known to man, known for breathability.

Velvet (Asia, Europe) Twill or satin weave fabric with a thick, short pile, originally silk. Thought to be brought to Europe along the Silk Road, perfected in Italy.

India

India is known for its early production of finely woven silk and cotton fabrics. The Kashmir region is well known for refined goat wool wovens. Surface decoration is highly prized in India. Folk embroideries incorporating tiny mirrors, beads and knot work are applied in geometric or pictorial motifs. Floral and geometric borders woven into cloth are common. Batik resist and tie-dye techniques are applied to whole cloth or threads prior to weaving. India is perhaps best known for its intricate hand painted or block printed floral patterns.

Near East

Clothing textiles were created from cotton, imported silk and local wool. Many fabrics were lightweight. Woven geometric patterns, stripes or checks were based on twill weaving techniques. Garments were decorated with elaborate embroideries utilizing chain or cross-stitch techniques in white or multicolour bright threads. The neutral shades of natural wool, cotton's range of whites and primary colours created from local roots and spices created the colour palette. The intense red madder dye of the Near East was prized throughout the ancient world.

Europe: Nordic and Western

The Viking peoples of Europe are one of the few that count knits as one of their traditional textiles. Yarns created from animal hairs were used. Naalbinding, a form of knitting with one needle, was seen as early as medieval times. Motifs in both knit and woven textiles resemble snowflakes and stylized animals. The most famous of woven patterns from this area of the world would be tartan or plaids. These bold checked patterns of repeating horizontal and vertical stripes date back as far as 400 BC.

Europe: Central and Eastern

Like all traditional peoples, costume varied from region to region. In this colder climate woven wool, heavier fabrics, velvets and fur were used. Textiles generally had a white or black base. Decoration was embroidered or woven floral or animal motifs in red, white, blue, gold or black. Fine pleating, gathered lace collars and bell-shaped skirts were common in women's clothing. Men wore tunics and decorative vests inspired by Turkish invaders.

25

TEXTILE CULTURE
EVOLUTION OF TEXTILE DESIGN
GLOBAL TEXTILE PRODUCTION
A CALL FOR SUSTAINABILITY
CERTIFICATIONS AND LABELLING
DESIGNER SPOTLIGHT – MISSONI

5

6

5 Traditional European dress: Woman of Sogn, Norway, old engraved portrait. Created by Pelcoq after photo of unknown author, published on Le Tour du Monde, Paris, 1860.

6 European influence: Traditional Scandinavian knit patterns printed onto wovens. D&G A/W 2010.

SOURCING AND SELECTING
TEXTILES FOR FASHION

CHAPTER ONE: THE ROLE OF TEXTILES IN FASHION
CHAPTER TWO: MATERIALS
CHAPTER THREE: SURFACE DESIGN
CHAPTER FOUR: CONCEPTUALIZING THE COLLECTION
CHAPTER FIVE: SOURCING YOUR FABRIC
CHAPTER SIX: TEXTILES AND THE COLLECTION
SOURCING INTERVIEWS
APPENDIX

26

TRADITIONAL TEXTILES OF THE AMERICAS

Brocade (Asia, South America)
Highly decorative woven fabric in which a compact warp effect background utilizes float weft fills to create a raised pattern. Chinese brocades featured silver and gold threads on silks, Mayans in South America used brightly dyed cotton yarns on a back strap loom.

Serape (Central America)
Originally woven from yucca, palm or maguey fibres, then eventually cotton. Striped or geometric patterned textile with a hole for the head and fringed ends. Often dark with bands of bright colours.

North America

The native tribes of North America relied heavily on animal skins for clothing. Always respecting the whole animal, the basic hide silhouettes were sewn together with bone needles and gut thread. Pieces were highly decorative with fringe, tassels, feathers, braiding and intricate porcupine quill or seashell beading. Motifs were symbolic of their connection to the natural world and portrayed celestial or animal images. Many designers today reference imagery from woven or quilted Navajo rugs and blankets or Northwest coast Chilkat hand-woven ceremonial capes and hand-carved totem poles.

South and Central America

The native peoples of South and Central America believed clothing could transform a person. They are known for their brightly coloured, highly patterned and decorated cloth. Ikat weaving, found in many areas of the globe, was particularly advanced, both in multicolour application and patterning. The patterns were precisely controlled on a back strap loom by wrapping the warp threads around a stick. Other methods of textile decoration included brocade weaving, tapestry, embroidery and tie-dye. Much of these lands are covered in lush rainforest. The proliferation of mineral, animal and plant has given these peoples a spectrum of natural dyes including lime greens, bright pinks, indigo – the entire rainbow. Imagery denoted status, religion and village through both design and colour. Motifs were often people, plants or animals.

27

TEXTILE CULTURE
EVOLUTION OF TEXTILE DESIGN
GLOBAL TEXTILE PRODUCTION
A CALL FOR SUSTAINABILITY
CERTIFICATIONS AND LABELLING
DESIGNER SPOTLIGHT – MISSONI

7 North American influence:
Fringe, beading and print
referring to native North
American tribes walked the
runway at Anna Sui's autumn
2008 show.

8 Traditional North American
dress: Photo of Kalispel girl, first
nation's tribe of Canada.

9 Traditional South and Central
American dress: Mayan vendor
in traditional garb at market.

10 South and Central American
influence: Mayan inspired
embroidery on the runway S/S
2008 Matthew Williamson.

SOURCING AND SELECTING
TEXTILES FOR FASHION

CHAPTER ONE: THE ROLE OF TEXTILES IN FASHION
CHAPTER TWO: MATERIALS
CHAPTER THREE: SURFACE DESIGN
CHAPTER FOUR: CONCEPTUALIZING THE COLLECTION
CHAPTER FIVE: SOURCING YOUR FABRIC
CHAPTER SIX: TEXTILES AND THE COLLECTION
SOURCING INTERVIEWS
APPENDIX

28

1 Textile production has moved from Europe to Asia.

GLOBAL TEXTILE PRODUCTION

As we have seen, all peoples of the world have produced their own textiles. Each area has had a unique focus in raw materials and decoration and yet construction methods tend to have many commonalities. Traditional textiles remain important cultural signifiers in almost every country. In the past few decades the world has become more easily connected and many new global areas have started to industrialize. Textile and fashion production has followed the path of cheaper labour and less stringent laws to these new manufacturing centres. Many traditional mills and artisanal studios are struggling to remain open and compete.

What it was

Throughout the history of textiles and fashion there has been a dominance of European fashion in modern society. As Europe, and then the United States, started to innovate in industrial textile manufacturing from the mid-1600s onward, the high quality, high tech resulting fabrics were produced in these areas of the world. For the past four centuries or so this is where most of the western world has looked to procure fashion textiles and clothing.

Certain countries in Europe and states in the US held much of the production capabilities with each being known for specific textile and fashion goods. In Italy many small to mid size factories produced fashion apparel in the north and textiles in the south. Naples was particularly known for the specialized manufacture of leather fashion goods. France has been known as the world leader in fashion design, particularly haute couture. Its production of textile products remained competitive due to the high quality and brand association. The UK continued to be a technological innovator in the textiles fields and was known for clothing production until the late 1970s. The US continues to be a world leader in industrial textiles but fashion textiles and clothing manufacturing have been in a sharp decline over the past few decades.

29

TEXTILE CULTURE
EVOLUTION OF TEXTILE DESIGN
GLOBAL TEXTILE PRODUCTION
A CALL FOR SUSTAINABILITY
CERTIFICATIONS AND LABELLING
DESIGNER SPOTLIGHT – MISSONI

Textile production today

Significant migration of the textile and clothing industries out of Europe and the US started around 1978. Up until that point international trade restrictions, design, engineering, economy, and management and marketing capabilities kept the emerging, newly industrialized economies from taking over market share. A number of signifiers led to a move of production to first China, Hong Kong, Taiwan and Korea, then India, Turkey and Eastern Europe after 2005. These signifiers included a drop in consumer spending on clothing in advanced industrial countries, the economic recession of the 1970s, growth of chain and discount stores, an increase in seasonal fashion collections and items per year, and the invention and implementation of automated pattern cutting, electronic production machines and computerized systems within the industries. China's economic trade reforms of 1978, and the creation of the World Trade Organization, encouraged large textile and clothing firms in Europe and the US to restructure. To compete many began pushing domestic design and creativity yet subcontracting almost all manufacturing to the same low-cost factories overseas.

What the future holds

It is hard to predict where manufacturing will progress to as places like China and India become more economically viable. There already has been some movement to smaller, less developed nations like Cambodia and Indonesia. It is possible that growing awareness of environmental concerns and social responsibility will enforce greater global policies and, as standards of living rise worldwide, that market prices will even out. Some US and European mills are still holding on and others have started to reopen in an attempt to bring back jobs and manufacturing economies. In fact there has been a worldwide backlash against the cheapening of the fashion manufacturing industries. There has been a slow realization that transferring the technology and machinery to a new workforce does not make up for the intangibles of good fashion: knowledge of design, access to skilled workers, proper maintenance, and product specialization. Many countries and cultural preservation societies are working hard to preserve traditional arts and manufacturing centres from getting lost in the sands of time. As such it has become in vogue for designers and fashion mavens to resource these methods. It started with the fair trade movement of the 1980s, which imported traditional clothing from native peoples. Today fashion designers work collaboratively with native collectives on fabric design or whole fashion articles, combining modern design sensibility with traditional techniques. Meanwhile major designers like Anna Sui in the US have taken on local production as a personal cause. This style of design, while gaining traction, remains niche.

**SOURCING AND SELECTING
TEXTILES FOR FASHION**

CHAPTER ONE: THE ROLE OF TEXTILES IN FASHION
CHAPTER TWO: MATERIALS
CHAPTER THREE: SURFACE DESIGN
CHAPTER FOUR: CONCEPTUALIZING THE COLLECTION
CHAPTER FIVE: SOURCING YOUR FABRIC
CHAPTER SIX: TEXTILES AND THE COLLECTION
SOURCING INTERVIEWS
APPENDIX

A CALL FOR SUSTAINABILITY

As production and manufacturing of fashion raced to keep up with technology and economic migration, something got lost. In a short few centuries, clothing ourselves became a toxic business both environmentally and socially. Advances in chemistry brought about technically amazing industrial dyes and textile finishes with unfortunate noxious side effects. Corporate industrial growth has killed many smaller family or community-run enterprises and given rise to unsafe, unethical factory jobs. It has taken a while for governments to see the need for ecologically focused laws pertaining to proper disposable methods and waste management. Many countries do not have unionized workforces or good governmental oversight for human rights. Combine these factors with corporate greed and often desperate economic situations in newly developing countries and the world still has a long way to go to create a more sustainable, equitable fashion industry.

Greening your line

Some designers are resistant to the idea of going 'green' for fear of being boxed into a preconceived notion of what that means or simply because of a lack of interest. We as an industry no longer have the luxury of looking the other way when it comes to sustainability. Every new and upcoming designer should learn how to incorporate considerations for both environment and workers' rights into their work. Designers must learn to include these concerns as a practice of design from the initial stages of inspiration and concept onward.

One does not need to become a 'green' designer or have that be a lauded part of their line's branding to consider sustainability as part of the picture. At this point in time there is no 100 per cent answer to the sustainability question. Instead there are choices, combinations of factors and small changes each individual can make to help turn the industry towards a cleaner future. The best thing a designer can do is get educated to the available options in relationship to their customer and their product. Every stage of the design process, manufacturing process and product life cycle has an environmentally friendly alternative. Not every alternative will work for every designer or each individual product. However, as more and more fashion companies request and implement these options, they will become more readily available, cheaper and second nature.

31

TEXTILE CULTURE
EVOLUTION OF TEXTILE DESIGN
GLOBAL TEXTILE PRODUCTION
A CALL FOR SUSTAINABILITY
CERTIFICATIONS AND LABELLING
DESIGNER SPOTLIGHT – MISSONI

1 A farmer picks organic cotton in Afghanistan.

2 Natural dye production card from Noon Design Studio, Chicago, USA.

Social responsibility

In addition to material concerns associated with creating textiles and fashion items, one should also consider the human component of production. This includes everyone involved in the life cycle of a textile or fashion garment. One of the biggest concerns is factory workers' rights. Awareness in this area is of huge importance and the conditions at any manufacturing plant you work with should be considered. There are other less obvious ways to be socially responsible throughout the design process. Some companies focus on fair distribution of pay throughout their employee structure, implementing restrictions on the highest level of pay dependent on what the lowest wage earner is paid. Interns should always be paid the local minimum wage or be paid by a barter system of education in which some time is spent on learning, not on internship duties. Designers can choose to focus on locality of supply and manufacturing systems, keeping industry local or working exclusively with small vendors. Many production co-ops exist in newly developing countries that provide quality manufacturing and keep entire communities afloat. Corporate tithing and being involved in events or programmes that give back to the community, when built into the structure of a business from ground up, become part of the overhead equation.

On the other end designers can work to educate consumers about care of their product. Often the environmental impact of garment care dwarfs the impact of creating both the textile and the product. By clearly labelling for best washing processes designers can help change consumer habits (Fletcher, 2008, pp. 76–92). Designers may also choose to clearly highlight some of the choices they have made that create a positive impact. By educating the public to the wider system of positive choice, we allow for a complete system change.

GOING GREEN
Five Easy Questions to Get You Started

1 Who? – 'Who?' pertains to all the people involved in your manufacturing and supply lines. If you are manufacturing or sourcing locally it is advisable to stop by the facility and check to see if you are comfortable with the working conditions. It's also appropriate to ask about hours, unions and if workers are being paid a livable wage. When dealing with an overseas or non-local manufacturer, check websites for a social responsibility page or contact the company and ask for a copy of any certifications. Unionized work forces are optimal.

2 What? – The materials you use to create your garments are one of the easiest places to start with sustainability. Since there is no perfect answer to creating a 'green' product, a designer has many choices here. As a small design firm it's easier to get creative with up-cycling, recycled fabrics, natural dye options and sustainable surface design. If you are working for a large design firm or have a large production run, you'll have the advantage of lower prices for higher minimums. The wise decision is to go as sustainable as is affordable and makes sense for your product.

33

TEXTILE CULTURE
EVOLUTION OF TEXTILE DESIGN
GLOBAL TEXTILE PRODUCTION
A CALL FOR SUSTAINABILITY
CERTIFICATIONS AND LABELLING
DESIGNER SPOTLIGHT – MISSONI

3 Where? – When it comes to sustainability, local is the logical answer. Manufacturing and sourcing locally keeps economies afloat, saves on shipping and carbon footprint and allows one to know who and how a product is being produced. It is not always feasible to produce locally. If you must outsource to a different community or country, do your homework. There are many alternatives out there that can be just as rewarding as working locally. One great option is small, women-run co-ops started through micro-loan projects. The co-ops often utilize amazing artisanal skills, offer quality work and help keep entire communities employed.

4 How? – The question of 'how?' should be asked early and often throughout the design life cycle. By utilizing smart design and pattern layout much textile waste can be avoided. How a manufacturing facility deals with waste products can easily be researched by either checking their website or asking directly about disposal recycling programmess or certifications. As a small designer you can look into local textile recycling programmes and bring your waste clippings there monthly. Every step in the design life cycle of a product has a sustainable option; with a bit of research and planning, how to 'green' your line becomes second nature.

5 Why? – This question should be considered both before the design process starts and after the garment is completed. Why am I creating this product? Why will my customer value this product? It's necessary to investigate this question in order to add lasting value to your designs. By examining the 'why?', a designer can extend the usefulness or life cycle of a fashion item through innovative design, quality materials and emotional value. In turn, a highly valued fashion piece can help save us from drowning in a sea of throwaway, fast fashion.

**SOURCING AND SELECTING
TEXTILES FOR FASHION**

CHAPTER ONE: THE ROLE OF TEXTILES IN FASHION
CHAPTER TWO: MATERIALS
CHAPTER THREE: SURFACE DESIGN
CHAPTER FOUR: CONCEPTUALIZING THE COLLECTION
CHAPTER FIVE: SOURCING YOUR FABRIC
CHAPTER SIX: TEXTILES AND THE COLLECTION
SOURCING INTERVIEWS
APPENDIX

34

1 International Fair Trade logo

2 (opposite) Common laundry care symbols.

CERTIFICATIONS AND LABELLING

The textile and apparel industries are big business. Like all multinational manufacturing industries, the products and manufacturing processes are regulated by a system of certifications, tariffs, trade laws and labelling. Applying these global classifications can be a matter of preference or a matter of law. It is likely in this age of global connectedness and e-commerce that you will be sourcing, manufacturing or selling internationally. It is important that you become familiarized with these systems of international trade. Even if your company never works internationally, many of these systems are present and must be considered in your home country. Figuring out how to apply these classifications to your product can seem a daunting task. It is important to remember there is easily accessible information out there through business mentors, websites and governmental agencies. It is also helpful to remember that you only need to know the information that concerns your product and business directly.

Certifications

Certifications are voluntary classifications applied to a manufacturing process or product to ensure added value and quality. Product certification assures a product's performance and quality, and sees that it meets qualification criteria stipulated in contracts, regulations, or specifications. Manufacturing certifications certify a facility making sure they meet with generic management system standards (GMSS). GMSS are applied to any size business enterprise, public administration or government agency within the areas of quality management, environmental management or human rights management. Independent accreditation bodies determine all industry certifications. Accreditation bodies are governmental or private sector associations of international scope that develop evaluation standards and criteria. They conduct industry evaluations and expert visits to assess whether or not those criteria are met.

35

TEXTILE CULTURE
EVOLUTION OF TEXTILE DESIGN
GLOBAL TEXTILE PRODUCTION
A CALL FOR SUSTAINABILITY
CERTIFICATIONS AND LABELLING
DESIGNER SPOTLIGHT – MISSONI

2

GUIDE TO COMMON HOME LAUNDERING AND SYMBOLS

DOS/WIN Code Ref#	Care Symbol	Written Care Instructions	What Care Symbol and Instructions Mean
WASH MW_Norm		Machine Wash, Normal	Garment may be laundered through the use of hottest available water, detergent or soap, agitation, and a machine designed for this purpose.
MW30C	30C	Machine Wash, Cold	Initial water temperature should not exceed 30C or 65 to 85F.
MW40C	40C	Machine Wash, Warm	Initial water temperature should not exceed 40C or 105F.
MW50C	50C	Machine Wash, Hot	Initial water temperature should not exceed 50C or 120F.
MW60C	60C	Machine Wash, Hot	Initial water temperature should not exceed 60C or 140F.
MW70C	70C	Machine Wash, Hot	Initial water temperature should not exceed 70C or 160F.
MW95C	95C	Machine Wash, Hot	Initial water temperature should not exceed 95C or 200F.
MW_Pres		Machine Wash, Permanent Press	Garment may be machine laundered only on the setting designed to preserve Permanent Press with cool down or cold rinse prior to reduced spin.
MW_Gentl		Machine Wash, Gentle or Delicate	Garment may be machine laundered only on the setting designed for gentle agitation and/or reduced time for delicate items.
Hndw		Hand Wash	Garment may be laundered through the use of water, detergent or soap and gentle hand manipulation.
W_DoNot		Do Not Wash	Garment may not be safely laundered by any process. Normally accompanied by Dry Clean instructions.
BLEACH B_Any		Bleach When Needed	Any commercially available bleach product may be used in the laundering process.
B_NonChl		Non-Chlorine Bleach When Needed	Only a non-chlorine, color-safe bleach may be used in the laundering process. Chlorine bleach may not be used.
B_DoNt_S		Do Not Bleach	No bleach product may be used. The garment is not colorfast or structurally able to withstand any bleach.

NOTE: System of dots indicating temperature range is the same for all wash procedures.

NOTE: All (98+%) washable textiles are safe in some type of bleach. **If bleach is not mentioned or represented by a symbol any bleach may be used.**

**SOURCING AND SELECTING
TEXTILES FOR FASHION**

CHAPTER ONE: THE ROLE OF TEXTILES IN FASHION
CHAPTER TWO: MATERIALS
CHAPTER THREE: SURFACE DESIGN
CHAPTER FOUR: CONCEPTUALIZING THE COLLECTION
CHAPTER FIVE: SOURCING YOUR FABRIC
CHAPTER SIX: TEXTILES AND THE COLLECTION
SOURCING INTERVIEWS
APPENDIX

Labels

Labels are internationally required on all textile and fashion goods but requirements and enforcement vary from country to country. Many countries carry strict penalties for non-compliance or label fraud. The system for textile labelling is standardized into categories. Every country requires at least some of these categories to be present on all textile goods. These categories are fibre content, country of origin, care, size and manufacturer/importer information. Each country also has a label language requirement. All these requirements can be best found out by checking with your import agency or government trade authority. In addition to the above categories, the United States requires all labels for the manufacture, importation, distribution and sale of textile, wool or fur products to have a business name or registered identification number (RN) present.

Tariffs and trade laws

Tariffs and trade laws are set by an individual government or by agreement among governments. It is important to be informed about tariffs and trade laws as they will directly impact your business's bottom line. Tariffs are taxes collected by a government on the value of an imported product including freight and insurance. In addition you may have to pay national and local sales taxes or customs fees. You must also be aware of the taxes owed if operating locally, as every major city, county, state or province has their own system of duties required on textile and apparel. Trade laws define the rules and customs for handling trade between countries. These rules change from country to country and product to product depending on the relationship between governments, certification requirements and local laws.

37

TEXTILE CULTURE
EVOLUTION OF TEXTILE DESIGN
GLOBAL TEXTILE PRODUCTION
A CALL FOR SUSTAINABILITY
CERTIFICATIONS AND LABELLING
DESIGNER SPOTLIGHT – MISSONI

HELP TO GET YOU STARTED

Often times the business end of fashion can be really overwhelming to the creative mind. However, if you plan on working for yourself or having your own line it will most likely be necessary for you to be involved on the business end of things. With a little research and time, it can be a lot easier then it looks. Reaching out to the many trade organizations, government programmes and business connections listed in the back of this book can help. Below are some places to start looking.

Certifications

Certifications are important because they allow you to be confident in the quality of the textile, sample or production run you are purchasing. They also allow you to make sure any facility you are working with employs certain standards for quality, environment and social responsibility.

ISO: International Organization for Standardization – the world's largest developer and publisher of international standards. Works independently with 164 countries. Offers many certifications of both products and management. Below are three to watch for:

• ISO-9001 – Quality management
• ISO-14001 – Environmental management
• ISO – 26000:2010 – Guidance on social responsibility
– www.iso.org

ASTM International – Independent accreditation body internationally recognized for product certifications. Search website for textile standards on: apparel, sizing, textile properties, specific fabric types, textile testing, finishes and labels – www.astm.org

Ecolabel Index – Online global directory of eco-certifications, lists over 400 independent standards in 246 countries. It's a good idea to work with companies that qualify for some of these as well as the ISO standards – www.ecolabelindex.com

Labels

Labels are required by international laws for all textile and apparel products. Since failure to comply with penalties can include stiff fines or even jail, it's a good idea to label your product correctly.

US: Dept of Commerce; International Trade Administration; Office of Textiles and Apparel (OTEXA) – government agencies that have all the information you would need for international trade of textiles or apparel. Search site for labelling requirements – http://otexa.ita.doc.gov

UK: Department for Business Innovation and Skills – government agency created to support business growth and skills in UK. Search site for textile labelling regulations – www.bis.gov.uk

Tariffs and trade laws

How these are applied and what's required vary country to country. The average world standard tariff is about 5% but other taxes and fees may apply. If you don't calculate these into product cost, you lose money! It's best to contact your freight forwarder or government agency when doing international trade.

US: Export.gov – official online resource that brings together resources from across the US government to aid businesses in international business success. Great information and resources for all international trade – www.export.gov

UK and EU: Business Link – the government's online resource for businesses of all sizes providing information, support and services. Look into international trade section. Great online questionnaire to help calculate taxes on import/export – www.businesslink.gov.uk

Missoni is the family-owned Italian fashion house synonymous with knitwear. Over a century of family business experience, both creative and technical, combined to create this innovative brand, first labelled Missoni in 1968. The brand is known for using a multitude of fibres and creating colourful patterns in chevrons, geometrics, stripes and stylized florals. Their patterns have become so iconic they have graced collaborative projects from bicycles to home goods to a hotel venture.

DISCUSSION QUESTIONS

1

Missoni is not only a long-standing fashion house but also a family business. Would you find this type of situation freeing or restrictive as a designer?

2

What do you think are the advantages of having a signature textile look? Are there disadvantages?

3

Do you think a great textile can carry a mediocre fashion design? Do you think an outstanding fashion design can elevate a mediocre textile?

4

Rosita Missoni's method is to work on the textiles first and the fashion designs second. Is this a direction that works for you in your design process?

Vintage Missoni knit. The Missoni brand
is known for its chevrons, geometrics,
stripes and stylized florals.

CHAPTER TWO

Materials

Textiles are the base materials from which a fashion collection is created. Within the field of textile manufacturing there are five basic steps that all or most textiles will follow before being becoming available to market. The steps are: fibres, yarns, construction method, dyeing and finishing. As technology increases some stages may be skipped due to new chemical base materials and innovative production methods. Likewise, as the industry looks further into sustainability issues, the market for raw, undyed or untreated fabrics has increased. However, the vast majority of fashion fabrics will pass through each one of these stages.

Every stage in the production life cycle of a textile will have a bearing on end cost to the designer. Each one will affect the properties, functions and durability of the textile and the resulting garment. Inherent from the fibre stage will be preconceived notions as to value, meaning and image. The exact same ball gown made from a poly-satin will be undervalued compared to the one made of an organic hand-loomed silk, even if they look identical to the untrained eye. How you plan out your seasonal collections to suit your target market and brand image has everything to do with understanding the five stages of textile production.

Design is a plan for arranging elements in such a way as best to accomplish a particular purpose
Charles Eames

SOURCING AND SELECTING
TEXTILES FOR FASHION

CHAPTER ONE: THE ROLE OF TEXTILES IN FASHION
CHAPTER TWO: MATERIALS
CHAPTER THREE: SURFACE DESIGN
CHAPTER FOUR: CONCEPTUALIZING THE COLLECTION
CHAPTER FIVE: SOURCING YOUR FABRIC
CHAPTER SIX: TEXTILES AND THE COLLECTION
SOURCING INTERVIEWS
APPENDIX

42

FINDING SUSTAINABLE FABRICS

There is a common assumption that natural fibres automatically create the most sustainable textiles. In part this can be true but as with most issues, creating a sustainable textile is much more faceted than a one approach answer. In order to assess the sustainability of a fibre for textile production one must look beyond its narrow classification into other areas such as:

• Energy consumption in the growth or manufacturing stage

• Processes required to extract or create a workable textile fibre from original source

• Social and environmental toll

• Necessity of dye or finishing to final end product

• Longevity or durability of resulting textile from fibre

• Care requirements of the final product

• Feasibility of recycle or disposal methods.

By taking into consideration all of these factors, what you find as a sustainable fabric for your line may surprise you.

FIBRES

Fibres are the base material that all textiles are made from. Originally there were only naturally occurring fibres, created from animal, plant and mineral origins. Since the Industrial Revolution, chemically created fibre stuffs from many different sources, both naturally occurring and man-made, have increased the pool of textile materials. No matter how many additional materials are manipulated in a workable fibre for textile production, the two basic classifications remain as natural fibres or man-made fibres.

All fibres for textile manufacturing have a flexible shape due to a high-length-to width ratio, resulting in a hair-like structure. This one characteristic is essential in an end product that must bend with the manoeuvrability of, and conform to, the organic shape of the human body. Within this common strand formation, it is the fibre's molecular composition and extraneous characteristics of length, surface, diameter and shape that determine much of the resulting textile's properties.

43

FIBRES
YARNS
TEXTILE CONSTRUCTION METHODS
COLOURING THE FABRIC
FINISHING METHODS
DESIGNER SPOTLIGHT – PATAGONIA

1

No one fibre, regardless of whether it is organic, fairly traded or recycled, can single handedly transform the practices of a polluting and resource-intensive industry into a more sustainable one.
Kate Fletcher, *Sustainable Fashion and Textiles*

1 Knit dress created from organic cotton, belt from woven raffia. Created by student designer Brian Nussbaum for sustainable design course.

**SOURCING AND SELECTING
TEXTILES FOR FASHION**

CHAPTER ONE: THE ROLE OF TEXTILES IN FASHION
CHAPTER TWO: MATERIALS
CHAPTER THREE: SURFACE DESIGN
CHAPTER FOUR: CONCEPTUALIZING THE COLLECTION
CHAPTER FIVE: SOURCING YOUR FABRIC
CHAPTER SIX: TEXTILES AND THE COLLECTION
SOURCING INTERVIEWS
APPENDIX

44

Natural fibres

Natural fibres come from animal, plant or mineral sources. Animal fibres are protein based while plant fibres are cellulosic. Some man-made fibres can also be cellulosic, starting with organic plant matter but chemically altered and classified as manufactured fibre. Protein fibres are gathered from the fur of an animal with the exception of silk. Silk is spun into a cocoon by a worm and can be extracted in a continuous thread. Cellulose fibres come from the seedpod, stalk or leaf of a plant. Asbestos, a toxic mineral used as a fire retardant up until the 1980s, is the only naturally occurring mineral fibre.

The oldest and most commonly used protein fibre is wool. Wool is shorn from either a sheep or a goat. The age of the animal, stage growth of the fleece and breed of the animal will affect the wool produced. The highest quality wools come from merino sheep or the second undercoat fleece common in several breeds of goat, known as cashmere. Other common protein fibres are mohair (angora goat), alpaca, angora (angora rabbit) and lambswool (unweaned sheep). Fibres from animals carry forth the traits that help maintain body temperature and water resistance in the animals they originally protect, but often have very specific care requirements in the final product.

Cotton is the most commonly used cellulose fibre along with synthetic polyester, accounts for 80 per cent of the global market in textiles (Simpson, 2006). Cotton fibre is gathered from the seedpod of the cotton plant and needs to be combed or carded to remove seed debris before being spun into yarn. Cotton fibres are extremely versatile, used in knit and woven textiles and are easy to dye, comfortable to wear and inexpensive to care for. Other fibres from seedpods, coir and kapok, are used only in limited treatments. Baste fibres are plant fibres that are stripped from the plant stalk in a biological process called retting. The oldest and most common of these is linen from the flax plant. Other common baste fibres are hemp, ramie, jute and bamboo. Baste fibres tend to be lower in elongation than cotton and create stronger textiles with breathability and moisture wicking properties. These fibres function well in woven fabrics but must be less than 50 per cent blend for knit. Knit bamboo has been chemically altered to create a viscose fibre appropriate for knit fabrics. Cellulose fibres may also be extracted from plant leaves but the end products are more often for industrial use.

45

FIBRES
YARNS
TEXTILE CONSTRUCTION METHODS
COLOURING THE FABRIC
FINISHING METHODS
DESIGNER SPOTLIGHT – PATAGONIA

2

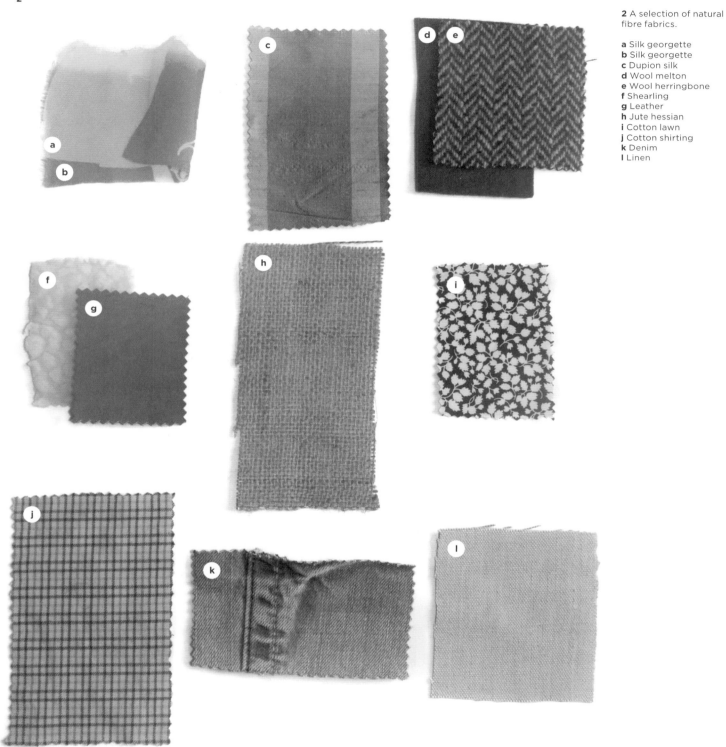

2 A selection of natural fibre fabrics.

a Silk georgette
b Silk georgette
c Dupion silk
d Wool melton
e Wool herringbone
f Shearling
g Leather
h Jute hessian
i Cotton lawn
j Cotton shirting
k Denim
l Linen

**SOURCING AND SELECTING
TEXTILES FOR FASHION**

CHAPTER ONE: THE ROLE OF TEXTILES IN FASHION
CHAPTER TWO: MATERIALS
CHAPTER THREE: SURFACE DESIGN
CHAPTER FOUR: CONCEPTUALIZING THE COLLECTION
CHAPTER FIVE: SOURCING YOUR FABRIC
CHAPTER SIX: TEXTILES AND THE COLLECTION
SOURCING INTERVIEWS
APPENDIX

46

Manufactured and synthetic fibres

Production of man-made fibres has been under consideration since 1664. However a useful textile filament was not produced until the end of the nineteenth century. This first man-made fibre, rayon, was produced by chemically altering cellulose material and forcing it through small holes, creating continuous strands of fibre. The resulting fabric was billed as 'artificial silk' and by the end of the twentieth century this fibre earned a 70 per cent US market share. Rayon and acetate, both altered cellulose, are the historic manufactured fibres. In recent decades, as focus has shifted towards sustainable fibre production, the textile world has looked back at trying to create new fibres from plant or animal origin. The new term for these fibres is **regenerated** rather than manufactured but they belong in the same category. The manufacturing process of these 'natural' materials utilizes a lot of energy and harmful chemicals on the way to becoming a fibre. Often the environmental benefits of these new fabrics come from sustainable and regenerative growth of the plants or animals involved, and a new form of closed loop processing that allows for a vast reduction in environmental waste. However, whether these benefits are used in production varies from manufacturer to manufacturer and country to country. Newly manufactured cellulose-based textiles include lyocell/Tencel®, Modal®, Viscose® and bamboo. Regenerative protein-based fibres come from either plant proteins (soy, corn, peanut) or animal proteins (casein found in milk). All filaments of these regenerated fibres are still produced by forcing a liquefied substance through a spinneret machine to form strands (Lackman, 2008).

3 A selection of man-made fabrics.

a Lyocel
b Nylon/elastene
c Nylon ripchord
d Nylon fusing
e Viscose
f Polyamide
g Polyester
h Polyester wadding
i Nylon
j Acrylic/wool
k Metallic silk

FIBRES
YARNS
TEXTILE CONSTRUCTION METHODS
COLOURING THE FABRIC
FINISHING METHODS
DESIGNER SPOTLIGHT – PATAGONIA

3

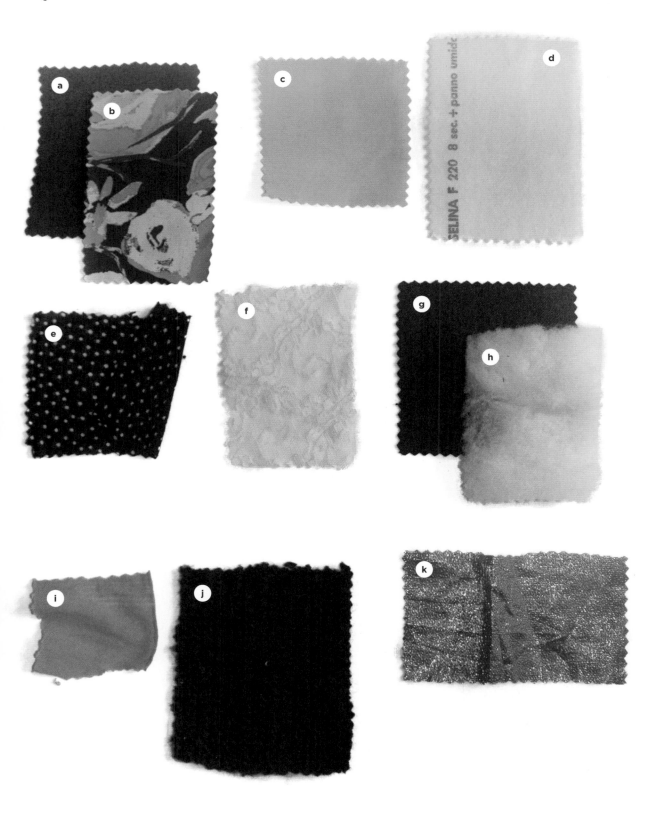

**SOURCING AND SELECTING
TEXTILES FOR FASHION**

CHAPTER ONE: THE ROLE OF TEXTILES IN FASHION
CHAPTER TWO: MATERIALS
CHAPTER THREE: SURFACE DESIGN
CHAPTER FOUR: CONCEPTUALIZING THE COLLECTION
CHAPTER FIVE: SOURCING YOUR FABRIC
CHAPTER SIX: TEXTILES AND THE COLLECTION
SOURCING INTERVIEWS
APPENDIX

48

Synthetic fibres differ from manufactured fibres in that they are completely formed from petrochemicals in a chemical process. Nylon, produced by DuPont in the 1930s, was the world's first synthetic fibre, followed closely by acrylic. The most popular of synthetic fashion textiles, polyester was discovered in 1833 but came into high fashion usage in the late 1960s. Synthetic fabrics are extremely popular due to the low cost of manufacturing and the durability and ease of care of the end product. However, since they are a form of plastic, the resulting textiles are not biodegradable, tend to melt at high temperatures and have very little breathability.

Speciality fibres are also categorized as man-made. Some are manufactured from natural origins and some are fully synthetic. Metallic fibres can be produced from many metals including nickel, copper, aluminium and super alloys. Historically gold and silver were spun into flexible textile filaments. Rubber can also be manipulated into a workable textile fibre. The synthetic version of a rubberized fibre called spandex was introduced into fashion clothing in the 1950s, revolutionizing the undergarment and swimwear industries. Microfibres are miniaturized synthetic fibres that measure less than one denier in length. They can be produced in a variety of sizes, shapes and synthetic combinations to create desired characteristics including odour resistance, hand, durability, moisture wicking and heat resistance. All of these speciality fibres are often mixed with other less expensive materials to produce affordable textiles.

49

FIBRES
YARNS
TEXTILE CONSTRUCTION METHODS
COLOURING THE FABRIC
FINISHING METHODS
DESIGNER SPOTLIGHT – PATAGONIA

4

4 1980s gypsy boho style dress created from sheer polyester. Vintage Diane Frels

Structural characteristics of fibres

In addition to a fibre's basic hair-like shape are five structural characteristics that affect the properties of the resulting yarn and textile. These can be categorized as length, shape, density, longitudinal configuration and surface texture.

Natural fibres are formed with specific traits inherent in their cellular structure and must be chemically altered or manufactured to change these five properties. One of the biggest advantages of synthetic fibres is they are engineered from the molecular level and can be given any variation within these five categories as well as additional characteristics.

Length – A fibre can measure less than an inch up to unlimited lengths for synthetics. Any fibre measured in inches is called a staple fibre, longer fibres are called filament fibres. Silk is the only naturally occurring filament fibre. Length of a fibre can affect texture, bulk, hand, quality and end use of resulting textiles.

Shape – Refers to the cross sectional shape of the fibre when viewed from its cut end. Shape of fibre will determine lustre/shine, bulk, texture and hand of yarn and textiles.

Density – Both the outer circumference and the inner fill of a fibre can affect a fibre's density. The bulkier the diameter of a fibre, the heavier the resulting fabric, while sheer, drapable fabrics are composed of finer diameter fibres. Natural fibres do not have uniform density while synthetics can be made uniform or non-uniform. Density can also be affected by the fibre being solid or hollow. Alpaca is a naturally occurring hollow fibre that helps with temperature regulation and dyeability in the final textile.

Longitudinal configuration – The varying configurations of a fibre's lengthwise structure are straight, crimped, curled or twisted. The two most common are straight and crimped. Crimp is inherent in wool and may be added to a synthetic. Increased crimp will affect warmth, absorbency, bulk, shrinkage and comfort on skin. All configurations will inform on resiliency, elasticity and abrasion resistance of final textile.

Surface texture – Each fibre has microscopic texture along the surface of the shaft. Some common surface textures are smooth, scaly, rough, grooved, wrinkled or channelled. The surface texture can affect permeability, stiffness, strength, dyeing, wrinkling, wicking and hand in the final product.

SOURCING AND SELECTING
TEXTILES FOR FASHION

CHAPTER ONE: THE ROLE OF TEXTILES IN FASHION
CHAPTER TWO: MATERIALS
CHAPTER THREE: SURFACE DESIGN
CHAPTER FOUR: CONCEPTUALIZING THE COLLECTION
CHAPTER FIVE: SOURCING YOUR FABRIC
CHAPTER SIX: TEXTILES AND THE COLLECTION
SOURCING INTERVIEWS
APPENDIX

YARNS

The next stage on the journey to creating a fashion textile is yarn production. Yarns are continuous strands of twisted fibres. All textiles are created from yarns with the exceptions of felt and non-woven fabrics (refer to pp 62 and 65). One fibre may be used to create many different types of yarn. How a yarn is composed can affect the final fashion product just as much as the fibre or the textile construction method. Much fashion trend analysis will start with yarn mills as the colours, textures and weights of the yarns being produced today will create the fashion textiles available in the coming seasons. These textiles will influence runway trends a year or so down the road.

Yarn categories

The two main classifications for yarns are **spun** and **filament**. Spun yarns are created from staple fibres spun together to create a continuous strand, while filament yarns are created from continuous filament strands. Because filament fibres are already continuous, just one fibre thread may be used, further classifying the yarn as **monofilament**, created from one strand, or **multifilament**, created from many.

Spun yarn is the classification for all natural yarns except for silk. Man-made fibres must be cut into staple length (measured in inches) in order to create a spun yarn. The fibres must have enough surface texture to create a holding friction when twisted together. Fibres are mechanically pulled parallel and then stretched and pulled in a twisting motion to create a yarn.

Filament yarns do not need to be twisted as tightly as spun yarns in order to have strength. These fibres are often given just enough twist to hold the multiple strands together. This enables the resulting yarns to create a textile with a smooth hand and lustrous surface. Technology has enabled the production of synthetic filament fibres even thinner than silk, yarns created from these **microdenier**, or **microfibres**, create highly drapable, silky textiles.

51

FIBRES
YARNS
TEXTILE CONSTRUCTION METHODS
COLOURING THE FABRIC
FINISHING METHODS
DESIGNER SPOTLIGHT – PATAGONIA

1 Spinning wool into yarn by hand.

SOURCING AND SELECTING
TEXTILES FOR FASHION

CHAPTER ONE: THE ROLE OF TEXTILES IN FASHION
CHAPTER TWO: MATERIALS
CHAPTER THREE: SURFACE DESIGN
CHAPTER FOUR: CONCEPTUALIZING THE COLLECTION
CHAPTER FIVE: SOURCING YOUR FABRIC
CHAPTER SIX: TEXTILES AND THE COLLECTION
SOURCING INTERVIEWS
APPENDIX

52

Yarn production

Yarn is produced by twisting fibres. Depending on the amount of **turns-per-inch (TPI)**, a soft twist or hard twist yarn is created. **Soft twist** yarns tend to be delicate with more loft. These yarns are ideal for knit textiles, offering comfort and stretch. The **TPI** is usually 2–12 turns per inch. **Hard twist** yarns have more durability and strength. The tighter twist creates a thinner, firmer yarn and they wear better in woven fabrics. Filament yarns are also lightly twisted but only to increase yarn thickness, as strength is inherent in the continuous structure.

Yarns are twisted in either a clockwise direction, creating a running spiral upward to the left or a counter-clockwise direction in which the spiral runs upward to the right. These spirals are referred to as **S-twist** (upward left) and **Z-twist** (upward right) as they resemble the diagonals in the letter forms. Twist direction affects appearance of the finished fabric but not properties such as strength, stretch or comfort.

Spun staple yarns are produced using one of three methods, ring spinning, open-end spinning or air-jet (vortex) spinning. **Ring spinning** is the most often used and creates a wide variety of high end, low production yarn types. **Open-end spinning** is used for high production, mass-market yarns of uniform texture and fibre distribution but lower quality. **Air-jet yarns** are limited to coarse, very fast production whose end use is suitable for sheeting, active wear and work clothes due to their anti-pilling characteristic.

53

FIBRES
YARNS
TEXTILE CONSTRUCTION METHODS
COLOURING THE FABRIC
FINISHING METHODS
DESIGNER SPOTLIGHT – PATAGONIA

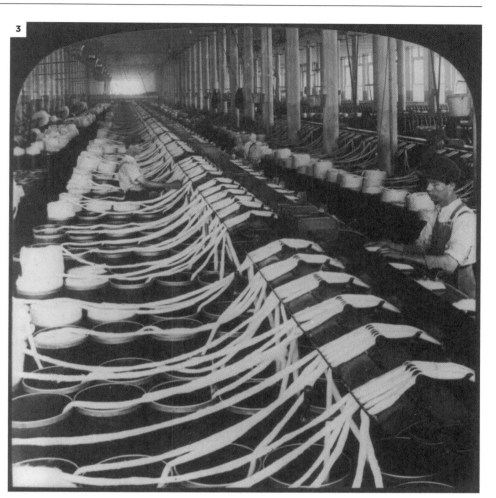

2 Woman working with spun yarns on a loom. Oriental Muslim National Crafts.

3 A worker at White Oak Mills in Greensboro, North Carolina makes cotton yarn, 1907.

Yarn types

Incorporating different combinations of fibre type, construction styles and production methods creates countless varieties of yarn. **Blending** two or more fibre types into one yarn is the most common way to achieve desired properties. **Plying** or twisting together two or more pre-existing yarn strands is another common method of strengthening, evening out diameter and improving yarn. Two-ply yarn indicates quality in the creation of fashion fabrics. Plying is often used in the production of **novelty yarns** in which metallic ribbons, common name **lurex**, or decorative strands with knots, beads, loops, curls and twist variations are plyed with a standard spun yarn prior to construction of fabric. **Textured yarns** are manufactured filament yarns manipulated during production to have an array of surface characteristics that result in desired fabric properties. Yarns with elastic properties are increasingly used in fashion fabrics. **Power stretch** yarns are used in swimwear and foundation garments, low recovery stretch yarns are used in **comfort stretch** fabrics utilized in everyday fashion, denim and active wear.

SOURCING AND SELECTING
TEXTILES FOR FASHION

CHAPTER ONE: THE ROLE OF TEXTILES IN FASHION
CHAPTER TWO: MATERIALS
CHAPTER THREE: SURFACE DESIGN
CHAPTER FOUR: CONCEPTUALIZING THE COLLECTION
CHAPTER FIVE: SOURCING YOUR FABRIC
CHAPTER SIX: TEXTILES AND THE COLLECTION
SOURCING INTERVIEWS
APPENDIX

54

When I don't have any ideas, I pick up fabric and start working with it and something happens.

Geoffrey Beene, fashion designer

TEXTILE CONSTRUCTION METHODS

Textiles are created by joining yarns in a variety of interlocking patterns to form a length of cloth. Along with fibre type and yarn category, the construction method offers the fashion designer important information for designing a collection. Inherent in every textile construction method is a basic set of fabric properties. Within each methodology is room for variation and expansion of secondary properties, but there will always be a core set of construction qualities. A good designer must know the basic qualities offered by each construction method as a starting point for realizing their vision.

Some designers source fabric for inspiration and allow the cloth's inherent properties to guide their work; other designers plan out their designs first and then search for a workable textile. No matter how a designer chooses to interact with the fabric, good design will always be based on choosing the appropriate marriage of material to vision. Woven fabric will be best for a tailored collection as it offers stability and structure; knits are best for active wear as they stretch and breathe with the body. However, by manipulating the fabric correctly a designer can achieve some degree of innovation over the cloth. A woven fabric cut on the diagonal bias will offer some stretch; an interfaced double knit can offer as much structure as a woven.

Woven textiles

The world's first constructed fabrics were **woven**. Woven textiles are formed by interlacing yarns set at 90 degrees to each other in a grid-like pattern. Vertical lying **warp** yarns run the length of a fabric, while horizontal **weft** yarns weave over and under filling out the cloth. Most woven fabrics are created with the use of a **loom**. On a loom the warp yarns are held taut and even spaced for the intended width of the fabric. A **shuttle** is used to draw the weft yarn over and under the warp yarns in a repetitive pattern. Along the lengthwise edges of the fabric a tightly finished strip called the **selvedge** is formed. All woven fabrics have a selvedge, which prevents the cloth from unravelling.

1 Selvedge denim seam finish on a pair of Cheap Monday jeans.

55

FIBRES
YARNS
TEXTILE CONSTRUCTION METHODS
COLOURING THE FABRIC
FINISHING METHODS
DESIGNER SPOTLIGHT – PATAGONIA

SELVEDGE AS A STANDARD OF QUALITY

The United States was once the main producer of quality denim: a durable cotton twill weave fabric.

In the early 1900s US denim was produced on 30-inch wide, hand controlled shuttle looms that used a continuous weft yarn to create a beautiful closed loop selvedge edge.

As technology advanced these looms were replaced by wider, higher production projectile looms that left looser raw edges on lower quality denim. Many of the old unused selvedge looms were bought by Japanese companies and transported to factories in Okayama, Japan. There, the traditional art of high quality denim manufacturing has been carried on ever since.

In today's high-end denim market, the most sought-after denim brands use selvedge denim created on these traditional looms. To maximize use of the narrow 30-inch cloth, the selvedge edge is used as a finishing agent on the outer seam of the finished jean. Denim aficionados and collectors often fold up the hem of their denim to reveal this sought-after selvedge mark of quality.

The fabric resulting from the weaving process is structured and has a repetitive surface texture. Its basic grid pattern creates two **grains**. The **lengthwise grain** follows the pre-stretched warp yarns and has good stability. The **crosswise grain** follows the horizontal weft and depending on how tightly these yarns are pulled against the warp threads, this grain will offer varying degrees of stretch. Most garments are cut so the stable lengthwise grain lies parallel to the body's vertical meridians. This cut also allows the cross grain to stretch over bending elbows, knees and buttocks. To achieve true stretch in a woven fabric, stretch yarns must be added or the pattern piece must be cut on an angle or **bias** to the grain. A true 45-degree bias offers the most stretch and drape.

Woven fabrics have a **face** and a **back**. In some woven cloth the difference in the two is obvious due to the weave pattern or finishing. These techniques can also create obvious **top** and **bottom** directional differences on the face. Designers must be careful even with plain weaves that appear reversible. Often manufacturing techniques used to maximize yarn quality on the face will reflect light and show wear differently once the fabric has been made into a finished product. It is important to always pay attention to grain and fabric side and direction when cutting pattern pieces.

There are three basic weave patterns from which all woven fabrics derive. By varying certain elements in these patterns such as fibre type, yarn gauge and twist, **yarns per inch**, and weave **floats,** fabric properties can be determined. Common woven properties are strength, lustre, drape, pattern/colour effect and quality/cost. **Plain weave,** in which one weft thread passes over one warp thread in a repeat, is the most used. Plain weaves offer an even surface for printing and wears well. **Twill weave** is formed by the warp yarns passing over and under two or more weft in a distinct diagonal repeat. A twill weave's short floats and compact interlacing create heavy, durable fabric. **Satin weave** creates a lustrous face by floating the warp yarns over four to eight weft but under just one. While offering added drape and beauty, this weave snags and frays easily.

2 A selection of
woven fabrics.

a Chambray
b Corduroy
c Basket weave waffle
d Towelling
e Voile
f Silk georgette
g Chiffon
h Linen/cottom
i Cotton gabardine
j Jersey
k canvas
l Satin
m Gingham
n Gingham
o Searsucker
p Cotton double gauze
q Cashmere
r Twill
s Plain weave
t Oil cloth

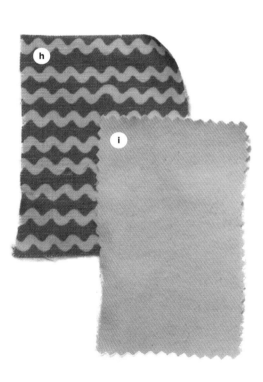

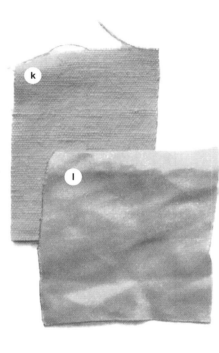

57

FIBRES
YARNS
TEXTILE CONSTRUCTION METHODS
COLOURING THE FABRIC
FINISHING METHODS
DESIGNER SPOTLIGHT – PATAGONIA

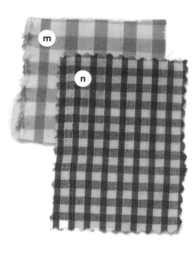

SOURCING AND SELECTING
TEXTILES FOR FASHION

CHAPTER ONE: THE ROLE OF TEXTILES IN FASHION
CHAPTER TWO: MATERIALS
CHAPTER THREE: SURFACE DESIGN
CHAPTER FOUR: CONCEPTUALIZING THE COLLECTION
CHAPTER FIVE: SOURCING YOUR FABRIC
CHAPTER SIX: TEXTILES AND THE COLLECTION
SOURCING INTERVIEWS
APPENDIX

COMMON WOVEN TERMINOLOGY

Basket weave – Weave structure that interlaces groups of two or more warp and an even set of weft yarns in a simple plain weave pattern.

Broken twill weave – A twill weave that runs with the diagonal pattern descending right for a certain amount of yarns then changes direction, creating an up-and-down zigzag often referred to as chevron or herringbone.

Clip-spot pattern – Small repetitive designs that are woven on the face of a fabric. Design threads are floated across the back surface to the design location. These threads may be clipped if the floats are too long. Swiss Dot is an example.

Computer engineering – The use of computer programs to quickly and inexpensively create, modify, present and manufacture woven fabrics, giving the textile designer and client a clear understanding of how yarn selection, colour, pattern and weave structure will affect final fabric.

Cut-pile weave – A weaving technique in which a third set of yarns going either with the weft or warp threads create a raised surface texture, which is then cut to create a luxurious texture. Velvet and corduroy are examples.

Dobby pattern – Simple repetitive geometric motifs created on a loom with a special dobby harness.

Double cloth weave – Two fabrics that are simultaneously woven and attached to each other by a separate set of yarns. Resulting fabric can be cut apart to form two lengths of fabric or kept together to create a thick fabric with two face surfaces.

Jacquard pattern – Complex and detailed woven patterns created on a special jacquard loom. Damask, brocade and tapestry are examples.

Leno weave – A weave technique in which weft yarns are firmly caught between spaced pairs of twisting warp yarns creating open, decorative, summer fabrics.

Rib weave – A plain weave in which the weft yarns are a thicker gauge than the warp, creating an obvious peak and valley pattern on the fabric surface. Poplin and taffeta are examples.

Uncut-pile weave – A weaving technique in which a third set of looped warp yarns create a raised surface. Terry cloth is an example.

59

FIBRES
YARNS
TEXTILE CONSTRUCTION METHODS
COLOURING THE FABRIC
FINISHING METHODS
DESIGNER SPOTLIGHT – PATAGONIA

3

3 Cardigan, top and bottom composed of different weight machine-knit textiles. Brochu Walker 2011.

4

4 Hand-knit sweater from the Conchula Collection by hand-knit fashion brand Pugnat.

Knit textiles

The second most common textile construction method is **knit**. Knit textiles are formed by interlocking repetitive loops of yarn. The loops are formed in rows with each successive loop passing back through the loop before it, forming a chain or a row of **stitches**. Knit fabrics are traditionally made by hand with the help of two stick-like **knitting needles**. Unlike woven fabrics, no special machinery is needed and hand-knit apparel items are patterned and formed as the textile is created. In recent years there has been a worldwide resurgence of interest in handmade knits, with everything from trims and accessories to complete hand-knit outfits showing up on the runways.

It is possible to create yardage of knit textile on machines and use it to produce cut-and-sew fashion items. Recently designer Issey Miyake has used computer engineering to knit fully formed patterned apparel on knitting machines (see Chapter 6, p. 172). The world's first **knitting machine** was created at the end of the sixteenth century. It produced a tubular length of knit fabric that was used to create hosiery out of cotton, wool and silk. Modern machines can produce tubular knit yardage on **circular bed machines** or open rectangular yardage produced on **flatbed** machines. A standard knit machine has 200 **latch-hook needles** and can produce fabrics utilizing extremely fine gauge yarns up to a standard **sport weight** yarn; **worsted weight** and **bulky weight** yarns require special machines for their weights. **Purl knit** and **plain rib knit** fabrics are created on **double flatbed machines**. Today's knit machines can produce any knit pattern or decorative stitch through computer control. Machines that utilize the **weft method** come closest to replicating hand knits but machines always create an even, repetitive stitch that separate their textiles from the organic beauty of a handmade item.

Due to the way knit fabrics are formed by chains of looping yarn (rather than straight pulled yarns as in a woven textile), the resulting textile is able to stretch in all directions. This one basic property makes knit textiles the fabric of choice for specialized fashion items like swimwear, sportswear, hosiery and foundation garments. Because of the general openness of the looped construction, knit fabrics can be made with loftier yarns and much heavier gauge yarns then woven fabrics. The added properties these soft spun yarns give knit fabrics are comfort, breathability and absorbency. A drawback is that the resulting textiles are prone to a much higher shrink factor when exposed to washing and drying than woven textiles.

Knit textiles have noticeably different 'right sides' and 'wrong sides'. The most basic stitch pattern is called **stockinette** or **jersey**. This stitch creates a vertical interlock 'V' pattern on the front and a horizontal wave pattern called **reverse stockinette** or purl stitch on the back. Alternating vertical columns of these two stitches create a **rib stitch** pattern that has extreme horizontal stretch. **Garter**, or **welt**, stitch is alternating horizontal rows with vertical stretch.

**SOURCING AND SELECTING
TEXTILES FOR FASHION**

CHAPTER ONE: THE ROLE OF TEXTILES IN FASHION
CHAPTER TWO: MATERIALS
CHAPTER THREE: SURFACE DESIGN
CHAPTER FOUR: CONCEPTUALIZING THE COLLECTION
CHAPTER FIVE: SOURCING YOUR FABRIC
CHAPTER SIX: TEXTILES AND THE COLLECTION
SOURCING INTERVIEWS
APPENDIX

60

5

61

FIBRES
YARNS
TEXTILE CONSTRUCTION METHODS
COLOURING THE FABRIC
FINISHING METHODS
DESIGNER SPOTLIGHT – PATAGONIA

DECORATIVE KNIT PATTERNS

Basketweave – Alternating checkerboard pattern of small rectangles composed of plain stockinette and reverse stockinette stiches.

Cable knit – System of raised knit patterns showing relief images of cables, braids, ropes, chain links and honeycombs.

Cardigan – A form of rib knit in which some loops are doubled so stitches appear to 'tuck' under each other. Creates a thicker fabric that is offered in full or half cardigan and appears the same on both sides.

Double knit – Hand or machine technique that knits two fabrics at once, resulting in two separate or one double layer attached textile. If attached the right sides face outward creating a thick reversible knit with almost no stretch in either direction and good shape retention.

Drop-stitch – Technique incorporating purposely 'dropped' or missed stitches leaving intentional runs or 'ladders' in an otherwise solid knit fabric. Creates a casual ripped lace effect.

Entrelac – Checkerboard effect of small knit squares attached by raised side edges.

Fair Isle – Named after a small island off the coast of Scotland, where it originated. This or less, repetitive pictorial pattern knit technique utilizes 'active' yarns on the face surface with 'floating' unused colours across the backside of the textile.

Intarsia – Multicolour knitting technique in which pictures are created on the textile surface. Unlike Fair Isle there are no floats but rather the yarns are cut and left hanging when colours change. Argyle is a well-known intarsia pattern.

Loop knitting – Technique where longer loops are drawn out of the knit pattern and knotted in place creating a shaggy surface texture.

Raschel – Warp knits created on special raschel machine. Raschel knit machines can create dense trim laces or open soft-spun lacy fabrics. Many different novelty yarns and stitches can be used offering a wide variety of decorative fabrics with an array of differing properties.

Tricot – Fine-gauge yarn warp knit textile. Soft, drapable, wrinkle and run resistant. Often used in lingerie and womenswear.

Tulle – Net warp knit with horizontal openings and a distinct body.

5 Knitwear collection by Japanese designer Everlasting Sprout S/S 2009.

SOURCING AND SELECTING
TEXTILES FOR FASHION

CHAPTER ONE: THE ROLE OF TEXTILES IN FASHION
CHAPTER TWO: MATERIALS
CHAPTER THREE: SURFACE DESIGN
CHAPTER FOUR: CONCEPTUALIZING THE COLLECTION
CHAPTER FIVE: SOURCING YOUR FABRIC
CHAPTER SIX: TEXTILES AND THE COLLECTION
SOURCING INTERVIEWS
APPENDIX

62

[In respect to materials] I have launched myriad novelties, even when the launching of them was hazardous – tree bark, cellophane, straw, and even glass.
Elsa Schiaparelli, fashion designer, 1890–1973

6

6 Tailored, felted alpaca jacket made from locally raised, hand-felted fibre. Fibershed Collective designers, Paige Green and Mali Mrozinski.

Other methods of construction

While most textiles are either woven or knit, there are other ways to construct a wearable textile. These other construction methods amount to a small percentage of worldwide textile production but have a lot to offer. Often textiles created from these methods are used in speciality fashion items as structural support or as decorative trims and panels.

Felt is the world's oldest textile. Felted fabric is formed from animal and/or plant fibres that have been exposed to heat, moisture and pressure. The resulting textile is sturdy, does not unravel and takes dye well. In fashion it is great for accessories or structured items.

Tufted fabrics are similar to pile fabrics in that a separate set of yarn is worked into a woven ground. However, tufting occurs after the base fabric is already formed allowing for more creative and decorative control. In fashion, fake furs are the most common tuft fabric.

Lace is a delicate and ornate technique of knotting, braiding and stitching threads and yarns to create pictorial, often floral, open-work trims and fabric yardage. True lace is created with a needle or bobbin method, though there are other techniques that mimic the lace effect.

Quilt textiles are created from two face textiles sandwiching an insulating fill. Puffed 'pockets' are formed by sewing decorative patterns that attach the three layers. Quilting has become a popular trend in outerwear.

Crochet textiles are created from a series of interlocking yarn loops. Only one hooked needle is used and wrapping multiple loops at once creates decorative stitches. Depending on yarn weight, fine lacy apparel to warm sweater weight fashion items can be made.

63

FIBRES
YARNS
TEXTILE CONSTRUCTION METHODS
COLOURING THE FABRIC
FINISHING METHODS
DESIGNER SPOTLIGHT – PATAGONIA

7 Fabrican Spray-on textile can be sprayed on top of moulds set directly on the body to create fantastic shapes and silhouettes.

SOURCING AND SELECTING
TEXTILES FOR FASHION

CHAPTER ONE: THE ROLE OF TEXTILES IN FASHION
CHAPTER TWO: MATERIALS
CHAPTER THREE: SURFACE DESIGN
CHAPTER FOUR: CONCEPTUALIZING THE COLLECTION
CHAPTER FIVE: SOURCING YOUR FABRIC
CHAPTER SIX: TEXTILES AND THE COLLECTION
SOURCING INTERVIEWS
APPENDIX

64

8 Hand-crochet apparel was part of the 'back-to-craft' fashion trend of the 1970s. Pattern photo for a maxi boho dress you could crochet yourself.

9 The non-woven textile, Tyvek®, was used to create this lace-like dress by Hila Martuzana for her project, The Rhythm of Paper.

Bonded textiles combine two textiles fused together with an adhesive. The backing fabric is often tricot and the face fabric is generally lightweight and inexpensive. The bonding process adds structure, value and durability to inexpensive fabrics that may not have been originally suitable for fashion apparel.

Laminated textiles are fabrics bonded with a sheet of polyurethane or other non-woven material. PU and PVC are two trade names for this type of textile in use in the fashion industry. These textiles imitate the look of leather and other skins and are common in accessories like gloves, shoes and purses.

Non-wovens is a category of textile that is not often used in fashion design. Non-wovens are formed by fibres (often recycled scrap) that are mechanically, chemically or thermally bonded into a web. Mainly you will see these materials in fashion use as padding or fusible interfacing. As technology advances some non-woven techniques have been used to design very artistic avant-garde items but they are not mass-produced. Often non-woven is assumed to mean any textile other than a loom woven one but this is not true. The title 'non-woven' refers specifically to the textiles produced from staple fibres of a certain length that have been bonded into a webbed fabric of a certain density.

FIBRES
YARNS
TEXTILE CONSTRUCTION METHODS
COLOURING THE FABRIC
FINISHING METHODS
DESIGNER SPOTLIGHT – PATAGONIA

If I am known for anything, it is my use of unusual materials. The origin of thought for many of my collections is materials, such as my Fall 2007 collection. Fabrics melded into each other, so one fabric became another, became another, became another. Sometimes, when you have simple shapes and you want to express profound concepts, you have to introduce complexity into your materials.
Miuccia Prada

Non-woven construction methods

Chemical bonding uses a chemical adhesive to bond fibres into a webbed porous textile.

Fusible fabrics are made from thermoplastic fibres or films; fusible non-wovens are the most used in fashion. These materials soften with low heat and bond themselves to cloth pieces offering structure and easy tailoring.

Mechanical bonding uses mechanized entanglement to bond fibres into a textile web; for example, needle-punched – a staple fibre web that is passed through a vibrating bed and pierced with barbed hooks to create a mechanically bonded felt-like textile. Used in apparel as insulation.

Sprayed fabrics are a web of cotton fibres that are sprayed out of an aerosol can directly onto the body. Once set the apparel formed can be removed, washed and dried. The brand Fabrican was developed by Spanish designer Dr Manuel Torres for Imperial College London and the Royal College of Art.

Spunbonded fabrics are formed from continuous filament extrusion into a bonded web. Known for producing a variety of differing weight textiles with a soft hand and drapability. Used for clothing interliners and protective apparel. Tyvek® is a brand name.

Thermal bonding uses heat to bond staple fibres into a fibre web; for example, melt-blown is a technique that breaks filament fibres into staple lengths which are blown and sealed by heat to a surface, used for insulation in boots and gloves. Thinsulate (TM) is a brand name.

**SOURCING AND SELECTING
TEXTILES FOR FASHION**

CHAPTER ONE: THE ROLE OF TEXTILES IN FASHION
CHAPTER TWO: MATERIALS
CHAPTER THREE: SURFACE DESIGN
CHAPTER FOUR: CONCEPTUALIZING THE COLLECTION
CHAPTER FIVE: SOURCING YOUR FABRIC
CHAPTER SIX: TEXTILES AND THE COLLECTION
SOURCING INTERVIEWS
APPENDIX

Non-fabric textiles

There are several materials used in fashion that function like a fabric but are not truly textiles. Some of these are the original textiles used to cover early man: leather, suede and fur. Others have come about in modern times, like paper and plastics.

Leather is sourced from animals. **Hides** are skins taken from bovines, horses or other large adult animals. The pelts of smaller animals like lamb, goat or calf are referred to as **skins**. Decorative skins can be sourced from lizard or amphibious creatures such as alligator or stingray. Leather needs to go through several processes to arrive at a workable textile. **Curing** by salt or drying so they won't rot. **Fleshing** to remove excess fat and meat from the underside. **Unhairing** to remove any fur, feathers or hair left on the skin. Finally **tanning** prevents rotting but also affects the properties of the resulting leather. Since leathers only come in the size of the animal they were sourced from, special consideration must be made during patternmaking to incorporate patchworking and piecework into a style. When cutting leather to piece together, attention must be paid to the natural **grain** texture on the skin's surface.

Suede is formed from leather that has been separated or **split** into two layers. The outer layer of skin is used to make high-grade leather but the underside is very supple and has a **napped** finish. This underside creates suede. Brushing can increase and smooth the nap to a velvet-like finish. The better quality suede comes from lamb, goat or deer. This quality suede is extremely supple with beautiful drape and it is often used in apparel. Pig hides and cowhides are also split to create suede but the resulting product is not as malleable and is more suited for accessories. Due to its porous texture all suede is easy to dye. Suede has a very distinct texture and look. While leather is something of a fashion basic, around every season, suede is not as popular and tends to come and go in fashion trends.

Fur is any animal leather with the hair still attached. As many animals become extinct or endangered, fancy furs, like tiger are often a common animal dyed to give the illusion of a rare fur. Many of the finer furs come from very small animals and so are often used as trims or must be patchworked. Small furs may also be cut by hand into continuous strips and knit like yarns to create textiles.

67

FIBRES
YARNS
TEXTILE CONSTRUCTION METHODS
COLOURING THE FABRIC
FINISHING METHODS
DESIGNER SPOTLIGHT – PATAGONIA

10 Many non-textile materials can be fitted to the human form and used to create outstanding fashion statements on structure, pattern and silhouette. Most of these looks will never be mass-produced. Mixed media dress by Iris Herpen, 2011.

Paper can be used as a textile for fashion. In 1966 Scott paper products sold dresses made of paper. They were an instant success and remained a trend for a couple years. While never a practical application due to susceptibility to tearing and water damage, paper as fabric enjoys a spot as a functional artistic textile. Since 2000 Japanese designers have been working with the traditional handmade paper washi to create washable, wearable yarns for textile creation (Swicofil, no date).

Plastics are man-made from petroleum. In fashion either flat malleable sheets are used as a textile or fibres are created for use in textile production. All plastics melt when exposed to extreme temperatures, some plastics will get stiff and brittle when exposed to cold. End uses of sheet plastics in fashion are raincoats, vinyl and outerwear; textiles formed from plastic fibres can have widespread applications.

Sourcing from animals: a question of ethics and environment

Fur has been dominating the runways for the past few seasons. This is somewhat surprising and a perfect example of how short a memory fashion can have. The fur industry took a huge hit in the 1990s with PETA's (People for the Ethical Treatment of Animals) anti-fur campaign. Since then the fur industry has tried to clean up its image, going so far as to bill fur as a sustainable answer to fast fashion. But while fur is indeed both natural and biodegradable, it is still sourced from living creatures that must be killed in order to supply the 'textile'. It is often in the manner of death, and the number of animals that must be destroyed to provide enough material for one fur coat, that for many designers the real question of ethics arises. As technology advances, the ability to replicate real fur increases, though sometimes nothing but the real thing will satisfy your vision. It is definitely worth investigating some of the information available to see how you feel about the use of fur for fashion (Penman, 2011).

People do not seem to react to leather as radically as they do to fur but there are a number of well-known designers that choose to have neither in their collections. Stella McCartney, Marc Bouwer, Vivienne Westwood and Olsenhaus are all examples of designers making this choice. In addition to animal rights issues, it is also worth investigating the environmental impact of the leather industry. Almost all stages of turning an animal hide into a wearable leather or suede product use environmentally and health damaging chemicals. The amount of petroleum, water and cleared land used to raise the animals far outweighs the amount of resources used to create faux leathers. There are some avenues to explore. Companies such as Ashley Watson Handbags and Olga Road recycle vintage leather to create their products. Natureally Organic Leather and Organic Leather are trying their hand at small farm, toxin free leather manufacturing.

11 The Super Twirkle Mini Dress by CuteCircuit is an interactive minidress utilizing smart technology. The fabric is embedded with CuteCircuit LED technology that sparkles and glows.

69

FIBRES
YARNS
TEXTILE CONSTRUCTION METHODS
COLOURING THE FABRIC
FINISHING METHODS
DESIGNER SPOTLIGHT – PATAGONIA

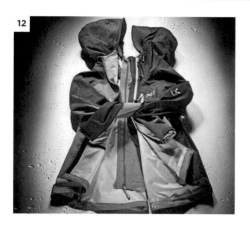

12 Breathe Easy Rab Stretch Neo Jacket with Polartec NeoShell (left) and Millet Trilogy Limited GTX with Gore-Tex Active Shell. Both Polartec and Goretex are well-known name-brand families of outdoor weather resistant fabrics created through fibre manipulation as well as coating and finishing.

Future fabrics

As technological advances are made both in fibre creation and production methods a new category of textile has emerged. These technologically innovative textiles are referred to as future fabrics. They are categorized by their special functionalities and hi-tech properties.

Nanotechnology is really the combination of science and textile production to create intelligent fabrics. These textiles are engineered on a nanoparticle level to treat or build fibres capable of releasing medicines, offering UV protection, detecting illness, and reducing body odour. While fashion has seen the use of nanotechnology for colour changing textiles, most of its applications are directed to medical use.

Smart fabrics are a form of nanotechnology. This is cloth that has electronic components. Microscopic fibrous particles that can perform electric activities, like monitoring bodily functions or lighting up, are merged with the textile. While still rare, some fashion companies are offering apparel made with smart fabrics.

PCM (phase change materials) are tiny microcapsules that can be trapped in the fibres of a yarn or textile. The microcapsules are filled with a solution that can change from a liquid to a solid state and back depending on outside temperature influences. As they change state, they enable the textile to moderate the personal body climate of the wearer, keeping them consistently comfortable even in extreme temperatures.

Thermal, waterproof, flame resistant textiles offer protective qualities often utilized in military and civil service apparel or the outdoor industry. Many of these protective qualities are engineered in at the fibre stage, such as the fire resistance of Kevlar® (an aramid fibre) or the thermal protection of Zero-Loft Aerogel (a flexible, silica gel-based material). Some are added through finishing such as Berghaus' hydrophobic down, coated with durable water repellent (DWR) (Weiss, 2011).

SOURCING AND SELECTING
TEXTILES FOR FASHION

CHAPTER ONE: THE ROLE OF TEXTILES IN FASHION
CHAPTER TWO: MATERIALS
CHAPTER THREE: SURFACE DESIGN
CHAPTER FOUR: CONCEPTUALIZING THE COLLECTION
CHAPTER FIVE: SOURCING YOUR FABRIC
CHAPTER SIX: TEXTILES AND THE COLLECTION
SOURCING INTERVIEWS
APPENDIX

70

1 Centuries old open-air dye reservoirs in a tannery in Fez, Morocco, where the world famous Moroccan leather is being made.

COLOURING THE FABRIC

Almost all fashion textiles are coloured through a permanent staining process known as dyeing. Dyeing can occur at the fibre or yarn stage, after textile construction or the textile may remain undyed until after garment construction. How and when the textile receives its colour can affect cost, sustainability, colour pattern, permanence and penetration of dye. Dye factories must be at the forefront of fashion trends, starting their predictions for colour and dye effects as early as three years before the coloured textiles are offered. Dye houses or vertically integrated textile mills with dye capabilities are responsible for most of the industry's solid and all-over dye effect yardage. Decorative dye techniques (covered in Chapter 3, p. 82) are often done by hand by textile and fashion designers on smaller amounts of yardage or finished garments.

Dye methods

Colour can be applied to a textile at different stages in the production cycle of a fashion garment. **Stock dyeing** is how fibres, generally wool, are dyed. The fibres are packed into a vat and liquid dyestuff is forced through, dyeing most or all of the fibres. The colour is evened out during later stages of production. **Dope dyeing** involves adding dye solutions to a synthetic mix prior to extrusion of filaments through the spinneret. Recycled fibres are also coloured. They retain colour from their previous life. When blending multicolour fibres or different fibre types the resulting fabric is **heathered**.

Yarn dyeing occurs after the yarn has been spun. The dye penetrates the yarn evenly and multicolours can be applied to sections of the same strand. Finished textiles are dyed by piece, batch or continuous dyeing methods. **Piece dyeing** is done by various methods on smaller amounts of yardage allowing for rush to market to keep colour on trend. More economical is **batch dyeing** in which ropes or flat widths of considerable fabric length are passed through dye baths. **Continuous dyeing** needs to process about 10,000 m of textile to be economical but can continuously dye 45.72–228.6 m (50–250 yd) a minute. The dye solution is fixed to the fabric with heat or chemical processes. **Garment dyeing** is the dyeing of a finished apparel item. Garment dyeing can make sense for a small designer who wants to offer a style in more than one colour but can only afford to purchase one roll of fabric.

71

FIBRES
YARNS
TEXTILE CONSTRUCTION METHODS
COLOURING THE FABRIC
FINISHING METHODS
DESIGNER SPOTLIGHT – PATAGONIA

2

2 There are many different, surprising ways to dye fabrics or yarns. This chart was made using the drink product Kool-Aid. Silk takes Kool-Aid as dye the best.

Natural vs synthetic dyes

Dye stuff can be made from many different sources. Basically anything that can be added to water in a high enough concentration to stain a fabric can be used as a dye. Different dyes work best on certain fibres. As a rule, natural dyes work best on natural fibres and synthetic dyes work on both natural and synthetic. **Natural dyes** are developed from plant, animal or mineral origins. These dyes come in a wide range of earth tones and a full spectrum of bright colours. While natural dyes have been used as long as man has been producing textiles, they have fallen out of use in modern mass production. Many artisans and small dye houses concerned with the environment are turning once again to the exploration of these dyes. **Synthetic dyes** are chemical based and can be mixed to produce any colour in any tone or vibrancy. Synthetic dyes have only been around for a little over a hundred years but they dominate the textile market. The emissions and run-off from these dyes cause intense environmental damage. If this is true why aren't natural dyes used more prominently in modern textile production? The answer lies not in a dye's ability to initially stain a fabric but in the **colour fastness** of the resulting textile. Many dyes when exposed to modern washing machines and detergents, light or perspiration cannot retain their original shade, uniformity or brilliance. While this is true for both natural and synthetic dyes, natural dyes are organic in molecular structure, not consistent like a man-made formula. This means it is harder to achieve consistency with natural dyes, they are less stable and more dependent on **mordants**, often chemical, to set the dye to fabric. However, interest in 'greening' the fashion industry has led to many advances in the use of natural dye for mass production as well as new environmentally sound **closed cycle** processes for synthetic dyes.

**SOURCING AND SELECTING
TEXTILES FOR FASHION**

CHAPTER ONE: THE ROLE OF TEXTILES IN FASHION
CHAPTER TWO: MATERIALS
CHAPTER THREE: SURFACE DESIGN
CHAPTER FOUR: CONCEPTUALIZING THE COLLECTION
CHAPTER FIVE: SOURCING YOUR FABRIC
CHAPTER SIX: TEXTILES AND THE COLLECTION
SOURCING INTERVIEWS
APPENDIX

TYPES OF SYNTHETIC DYES

Acid – Water soluble; used in batch dyeing of fashion textiles formed from natural protein fibres or synthetic nylon; as long as you do not inhale the dry dye stuff, succ reasonably safe for in-home use.

Cationic – Also known as basic dyes; water soluble and set with a mordant: best when used on acrylic fibres; not fast to light, washing or perspiration on other fibre types.

Direct – Also known as substantive; mainly used on cellulosic fibres like cotton and rayon; water soluble dye applied directly to fabric without use of a mordant; not bright or wash fast but light resistant.

Disperse – Not water soluble; used in continuous dyeing for polyester, acetate and other synthetics.

Mordant – Acidic in character; sodium or potassium bichromate is used to bind the dye; colour fast on wool, can dye cotton, linen, silk, rayon and nylon with less successful results.

Reactive – Water soluble dyes; largest class of dyes used in both batch and continuous dyeing of most textile fibre types; dye chemically reacts with the fibre molecules to form a chemical compound; textile must be washed to remove unfixed dye before wearing.

Sulfur – Insoluble without aid of caustic soda or sodium sulfate; utilizes high heat and salt additives to penetrate fibres; oxidation to air or chemicals bring about desired shades; used on cotton and linen; fast to light, washing and perspiration.

Vat – These are both natural and synthetic; water insoluble unless reduced in alkaline solution; oxidation to air restores dye to insoluble form; fastest dyes for cotton, linen and rayon; mordant is necessary to dye acrylics, polyester and cellulosic fabrics.

73

FIBRES
YARNS
TEXTILE CONSTRUCTION METHODS
COLOURING THE FABRIC
FINISHING METHODS
DESIGNER SPOTLIGHT – PATAGONIA

3

3 When accessories brand, Baggu, first began collaborating with dye designer, Shabd, these bags were hand dyed. 'She could only make about ten per day,' says Baggu owner Sugihara. Now the bags are shipped blank from China and sent to an industrial dye house in Los Angeles, where Shabd worked to teach the factory her process. Because they are the result of a two-part manufacturing process, the bags are a bit more expensive than Baggu's typical offerings.

**SOURCING AND SELECTING
TEXTILES FOR FASHION**

CHAPTER ONE: THE ROLE OF TEXTILES IN FASHION
CHAPTER TWO: MATERIALS
CHAPTER THREE: SURFACE DESIGN
CHAPTER FOUR: CONCEPTUALIZING THE COLLECTION
CHAPTER FIVE: SOURCING YOUR FABRIC
CHAPTER SIX: TEXTILES AND THE COLLECTION
SOURCING INTERVIEWS
APPENDIX

74

FINISHING METHODS

Finishing is the last step a textile goes through prior to market. Finishing refers to preparatory steps prior to dyeing or printing, dyeing and printing themselves, and any special properties applied to a textile through an external process after colouring is complete. While technology has enabled manufacturers to add some desired properties during all stages of the manufacturing process, others are more easily applied to the finished textile. Many practical and performance finishes, such as water resistance and stabilizing, are applied in a simple coating process, and most decorative finishes need the full canvas of a completed textile or garment to work on. Finishing typically takes place prior to garment construction but some finishes can also be successfully applied after.

Finishing in preparation of colour

There are **pre-treatment processes** that are used to prepare textiles to bond better with dyes or printing inks. These processes are done after textile construction is complete and clean the fabric of all impurities built up during the construction process. These impurities include sizing applied to yarns, oils, waxes and machine lubricants as well as general soil picked up in the manufacturing plant.

All textiles go through a laundering process called **scouring** (wool, worsteds) or **boil-off** (cotton, silk, synthetics) in which they are washed with detergents and dried. Woven fabrics with sizing are passed through a **desizing** enzyme bath to dissolve the starches. Knit fabrics that have had oils added to reduce static and soften the yarns are treated to a **solvent scouring** to remove them. If a fabric has fibre or filament splintering or projecting on the surface of the fabric these hair-like fibres are burned off in a process called **singeing**. This reduces the surface to its smoothest texture. This is especially important if the fabric is intended for printing. If a fabric is to be printed or dyed a light-to-medium colour, it must be **bleached** to a pure white. Most natural fibres are off-white to deep cream or yellow and this can affect the purity of the dye colour. In addition if the fabric is to remain white or be dyed a pastel shade an **optical brightener** must be added. This chemical process enables the fabric to absorb yellowing ultraviolet light and emit a cool brightening light.

75

FIBRES
YARNS
TEXTILE CONSTRUCTION METHODS
COLOURING THE FABRIC
FINISHING METHODS
DESIGNER SPOTLIGHT – PATAGONIA

1

1 In a rush to design the next big thing, the denim industry has pushed the creative envelope when inventing and applying aesthetic finishes to denim jeans.

**SOURCING AND SELECTING
TEXTILES FOR FASHION**

CHAPTER ONE: THE ROLE OF TEXTILES IN FASHION
CHAPTER TWO: MATERIALS
CHAPTER THREE: SURFACE DESIGN
CHAPTER FOUR: CONCEPTUALIZING THE COLLECTION
CHAPTER FIVE: SOURCING YOUR FABRIC
CHAPTER SIX: TEXTILES AND THE COLLECTION
SOURCING INTERVIEWS
APPENDIX

76

Finishing categories

Finishes are applied in one of two ways: mechanically or chemically. The purpose of finishing can be aesthetic or functional. All finishes have differing degrees of permanence. **Mechanical finishing** is applied physically to a textile or garment. These finishes are often **aesthetic**, enhancing or changing the look, drape or feel of the material. Many mechanical aesthetic finishes are achieved through washing, heat exposure, pressing, or brushing the fabric. The denim industry is a great example of mechanized aesthetic finishing. In recent years there has been a rise of innovative hand-done processes on blue jeans including sanding, localized bleaching, roller pressing, intentional ripping, waxing and hand-applied stains.

Chemical finishing is also known as wet finishing. Most of the chemical finishes are applied to fabrics in a bath and then are passed through padded rollers to press the finishing agent further into the fabric fibres. The chemical is then bonded or cured by heat drying. Some aesthetic and most **functional finishes** are achieved through chemical means. Many chemical properties have become commonplace: anti-static, anti-creasing and soil resistance, while others are more specialized such as waterproofing or ultraviolet-absorption. Typically specialized finishings are created for military or industrial purposes but fashion designers, especially in the outdoor lifestyle categories, often benefit from the use of these textiles.

There are four classifications of durability of finishes. **Permanent finishes** will last the life of the textile because the fibre structure has been chemically altered. **Durable finishes** will last but will become diminished through laundering until the finish is almost completely removed. **Semi-durable** finishes quickly fade after successive laundering but can be renewed in home laundering or dry cleaning. **Temporary finishes** are faded or removed with the first laundering.

77

FIBRES
YARNS
TEXTILE CONSTRUCTION METHODS
COLOURING THE FABRIC
FINISHING METHODS
DESIGNER SPOTLIGHT – PATAGONIA

COMMON AESTHETIC FINISHES

Acid wash – Used mainly on denim and jersey knits, bleaching process using chlorine and pumice stones to give a frosted appearance.

Calendering – Pressing a fabric in heated rollers to give a smooth, lustre finish, can be used to apply moiré patterns, embossed designs, high gloss glazes or a wet look finish called ciré.

Fulling – Creates a felt-like material out of a knit or woven wool through progressive shrinkage.

Mercerization – Improves the lustre, strength and dyeability of cotton through chemical finishing.

Napping/suedeing – Brushing the surface of a textile to give a raised textured surface. Suede is a finer finish than nap.

Softening – Can be applied mechanically or chemically to improve the hand and drape of a fabric.

COMMON FUNCTIONAL FINISHES

Anti-microbial – Increases stain and odour resistance and prevents the moulding and weakening of the fibres.

Flame resistant – Prevents fabric from catching fire quickly. In the US federally required for children's sleep wear.

Water repellent – Allows for air and moisture to pass through the fabric but repels liquids, for use in stain resistance or actual water repellent gear.

Wrinkle resistance – Also known as durable press; gives a permanent crease resistance to the fabric regardless of laundering.

DESIGNER
SPOTLIGHT
PATAGONIA

Patagonia is an outdoor lifestyle brand designing innovative and environmentally friendly textiles since the 1970s. It is one of the most well-known outdoor clothing brands. Its apparel range is well styled and functional but its textiles are what set it apart from its competitors. Patagonia custom develops textiles that are technologically advanced but always keep in mind environmental impact.

DISCUSSION QUESTIONS

1

Patagonia is a world leader in integrating eco-textiles into their collections. Do you think their commitment to sustainability has played a part in the success of the brand?

2

Patagonia is an outdoor lifestyle brand. Do you think other markets in the fashion world can make the same commitment to sustainable textiles with as much success?

3

Sustainability can be integrated into a line through many avenues. Textiles are just part of the equation. Can you think of other ways to make a line more sustainable?

4

Patagonia is also known for its technical textile developments incorporating properties like odour control, moisture wicking, and temperature retention. What technical performance properties would you look for in a textile for your collection? Why?

The polyester shell of this
Patagonia jacket is made from
recycled materials such as old
soda bottles, unusable second
quality fabrics and worn out
garments.

CHAPTER THREE
Surface Design

Surface design is an important part of the fashion design process. Surface design refers to any decorative treatment that enhances the overall look of a textile or garment. Surface treatments may take place during the manufacturing stage through the use of novelty yarns, specialized construction methods, and industrial dye effects or printing. However, many times decorative treatments are applied to a fabric or finished garment later in the fashion cycle by a textile or fashion designer. A designer can use surface design to increase value, tie a collection together, set their designs apart, interpret a trend or create a signature style.

There are many decisions to be considered when adding surface design to a fashion collection. Methods range from two-dimensional effects such as dye, print and paint to the addition of three-dimensional elements, fabric manipulation and embroidery. Any technique may be applied to create an all-over texture or pattern. Treatments can also be focused in one area to create a spot design or accent. A designer may choose to add surface treatments at the fabric stage, after pattern pieces have been cut or to the finished garment. Each of these decisions needs to be carefully considered by the designer as to added cost, appropriateness of technique to fabric weight and construction, final care of garment and whether the surface design is enhancing or distracting to the overall aesthetic.

We live in a web of ideas, a fabric of our own making.
Joseph Chilton Pearce

**SOURCING AND SELECTING
TEXTILES FOR FASHION**

CHAPTER ONE: THE ROLE OF TEXTILES IN FASHION
CHAPTER TWO: MATERIALS
CHAPTER THREE: SURFACE DESIGN
CHAPTER FOUR: CONCEPTUALIZING THE COLLECTION
CHAPTER FIVE: SOURCING YOUR FABRIC
CHAPTER SIX: TEXTILES AND THE COLLECTION
SOURCING INTERVIEWS
APPENDIX

1 Kumkum powders are natural dyes from India.

DECORATIVE DYE EFFECTS

Dye is one of the most versatile mediums with which to enhance the design of a fashion garment. Most textiles are dyed at some point in the manufacturing process and are offered for sale in a range of seasonal colours. Fabrics can also be purchased that have had no dye applied. These are called greige goods. Designers can choose to work with either previously dyed or griege textiles when applying decorative dye techniques to their work. If dyeing a previously dyed fabric you must be aware that the original colour will affect any additional colours applied. Bleaching agents may be used in a reverse dye method and can be applied decoratively to coloured fabric utilizing the same pattern techniques as dye to uncoloured fabrics. Designers or custom dye houses will work with textile yardage or finished garments to apply all-over dye techniques by machine or manually. Decorative spot dye techniques are more labour intensive and costly. A designer will need to work in-house or with a specialized vendor to achieve these hand-applied effects.

All-over dye techniques

All-over dyeing is achieved by adding dyestuff to a liquid and submersing the fabric or garment into the **dye bath**. Depending on the size of their production run a designer may choose to either work with dye on their own or send the work out to a custom dye house. It is important to understand what effect is to be achieved to know what types of dyes and equipment are needed. With a little research and practice, a designer can undertake fabric and/or garment dyeing in studio. However as their company grows they will need to plan for increased production either by growing in-house dyeing capabilities or lining up outside dye vendors for a smooth transition. One option is for a designer to create a sample in-house and then work with a vendor to recreate it for production. Many dye houses offer both machine and hand dyeing for fabric and garment in large or small runs. Some work with larger full production dye houses capable of recreating yardage of any fabric sample. While most of the industry works with synthetic dyes, a few production dye works can be found that focus solely on natural dyestuff and environmental processes. Specialized tie-dye studios can also be found that focus solely on decorative tie and dye methods.

2 Hand-tied
Kantano shibori
dye technique.

There are a number of all-over dye effects that cannot be achieved at mill dyed factories. **Custom colour** or over dyeing will change the colour of a fabric to a designer's specifications. Some dye houses only offer colours available in their seasonal **dye book** but many will offer custom colour mixing if a designer can meet minimums. When over dyeing pre-coloured fabric the original colour must be a number of values lighter than the desired end colour. Almost all pre-dyed colours will affect an over dye and truly dark colours cannot be over dyed. **Ombre** or **dip dye** effect can be used either as an all-over or spot technique. Sections of the textile or garment are submerged in successively darker coloured dye baths or are gradually left longer in the same bath creating a gradated effect.

Reactive dye is used to create full even shades. **Pigment dye** is applied in a unique process that creates a faded, washed look. **Low water immersion** technique uses very little water and adds the fixer last allowing dye to slowly spread and blend within the fabric itself. Beautiful and uncontrolled marbling occurs. **Crystal dye** creates a distinct shattered glass dye effect. Many dye houses offer specialized washes as well. **Mineral wash** can create a denim-like effect on non-denim fabrics and is easily modified to create many finishes. **Enzyme wash** softens fabric giving a worn-in look and feel (used especially with denim). **Acid wash** accelerates ageing of fabric and produces a frosted look. **Stone wash** uses pumice stones or chemicals to create uneven faded colouration.

SOURCING AND SELECTING
TEXTILES FOR FASHION

CHAPTER ONE: THE ROLE OF TEXTILES IN FASHION
CHAPTER TWO: MATERIALS
CHAPTER THREE: SURFACE DESIGN
CHAPTER FOUR: CONCEPTUALIZING THE COLLECTION
CHAPTER FIVE: SOURCING YOUR FABRIC
CHAPTER SIX: TEXTILES AND THE COLLECTION
SOURCING INTERVIEWS
APPENDIX

84

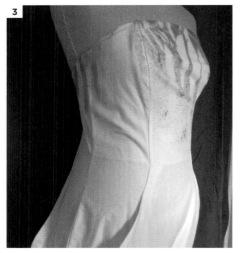

3 Hand-applied spray spot dye technique on a design by Erin Cadigan.

4 Multiple tie-dye patterns can be applied to one garment through careful planning.

5 (opposite) Ombre dye kimono. Alexander McQueen RTW S/S 2008.

Spot dye techniques

Spot dye techniques are applied to small amounts of yardage or to a finished garment. Working on a finished garment makes it easier to control where the dye effect is placed and to repeat it consistently throughout production. Any dye technique can be used to create an all-over effect but may not be cost effective. Spot techniques are labour intensive and therefore more costly. With advances in photorealistic printing capabilities it is not unusual to see traditionally labour-intensive dye techniques like shibori printed on a fabric rather than actually dyed. If these dye effects are used for a spot decoration or in minimal applications the beauty of the handiwork quickly adds value to a collection. Printing can never fully reproduce the unique, organic movement of dye.

Space dyeing yarns can achieve an all-over pattern in a woven fabric known as **ikat**. The same yarns used in knitting will give an organic tie-dye effect. There are two main methods of spot dyeing fabrics: direct application or resist. In a direct application process the dye is applied to the fabric in a controlled manner by using a variety of tools. **Splatter** or **drip** technique mimics the look of thrown paint or a drop cloth. **Spray method** may be applied with handheld spray bottles or larger airbrushes. Hand stamping or painting dye onto fabric is easily controlled when a thickener like **sodium alginate** or **monogum** is added to the liquid dye.

Resist dye techniques control the flow of dye to create patterns between the dyestuff and the original colour of the cloth. **Shibori** is a traditional Japanese method of resist dye work that uses binding, stitching, folding, and twisting to protect areas of the fabric from being dyed. The resulting patterns are very intricate. **Tie-dye** is a modern method of traditional resist dye techniques. The textile is bunched or folded then bound with string or rubber bands prior to dye submersion. The resulting patterns are less delicate and easier to achieve. **Batik** is a method in which wax or modern crafter's resist is applied to a textile. These substances bind with the fibres disallowing dye penetration but can later be removed from the fabric with heat. **Rice paste** may be used as a resist for quick cool dye baths or hand application. Potato dextrin cracks as it dries creating a beautiful lacy resist. **Potato dextrin** is easy to work with but cannot hold up to immersion, only hand-applied dye.

85

DECORATIVE DYE EFFECTS
PRINT AND PATTERN
EMBROIDERY
THREE-DIMENSIONAL SURFACE TECHNIQUES
DESIGNER SPOTLIGHT – ANNA SUI

5

SOURCING AND SELECTING
TEXTILES FOR FASHION

CHAPTER ONE: THE ROLE OF TEXTILES IN FASHION
CHAPTER TWO: MATERIALS
CHAPTER THREE: SURFACE DESIGN
CHAPTER FOUR: CONCEPTUALIZING THE COLLECTION
CHAPTER FIVE: SOURCING YOUR FABRIC
CHAPTER SIX: TEXTILES AND THE COLLECTION
SOURCING INTERVIEWS
APPENDIX

Art is the imposing of a pattern on experience, and our aesthetic enjoyment is recognition of the pattern.
Alfred North Whitehead

PRINT AND PATTERN

Pattern is created by the repetition of decorative elements applied through the use of colour, line and shape. *Print* can refer to either the process of applying an image or pattern to the surface a textile, or to the image created. Certain patterns can be formed during the construction phase of textile manufacturing. A wider variety of patterns and placed images are created for textiles through various print techniques. Designers may choose to source a patterned or printed textile for their collection from a mill, converter, jobber or retailer. They can work with graphic designers, textile designers or custom print houses to create or purchase signature prints for a season. It is also possible for a designer to utilize Computer Aided Design (CAD) programs and/or traditional methods to create their own repeat patterns and prints. There are many ways to apply custom print or pattern to a fabric, either by contracting out to a vendor or by working with traditional hand-print methods in studio.

Pattern

While most patterns are printed on a finished fabric some traditional patterns are formed during textile creation. Plaid, ikat, jacquard and damask patterns are all created on the loom. Tapestry method can be used to create a spot print or large-scale mono-image on a loom. Fair Isle and intarsia are knit methods used to create pattern.

There are many categories of printed textile pattern. Within any given category the elemental design features can be interpreted in myriad ways to create limitless variations on a pattern theme. **Polka dot** is the repetitive use of circles to create pattern. **Stripes** are directional bands of parallel lines. Printed **plaids** are intersecting stripes based on the 90-degree angles of warp and weft. **Geometric prints** can mimic structured woven patterns like houndstooth, check or chevron. They may also reference geometric shapes in abstract repeat. **Florals** are created from flower, grass or leaf motifs. This category is extremely popular and may be interpreted in many styles, for example, watercolour, mini, or art deco. **Conversational** prints are pictorial representations of everyday items. **Folk** or **tribal** prints mimic traditional art styles and fabric patterns from around the globe. **Ditsy** is any miniaturized, scattered motif. **Animal** prints refer to any pattern that resembles the skin of a living creature. **Paisley** (stylized floral), **chinoiserie** (Asian motifs), and **toile** (clustered pastoral scenes) are all common traditional patterns. **Camouflage** (abstract interpretation of scenery) and **psychedelic** (multicoloured outlandish prints) are commonly interpreted modern patterns.

87

DECORATIVE DYE EFFECTS
PRINT AND PATTERN
EMBROIDERY
THREE-DIMENSIONAL SURFACE TECHNIQUES
DESIGNER SPOTLIGHT – ANNA SUI

1

2

1 & 2 One pattern may be carried through a collection in varying sizes and colours to create interest. Polka dot parade seen at Luella Bartley S/S 2010.

**SOURCING AND SELECTING
TEXTILES FOR FASHION**

CHAPTER ONE: THE ROLE OF TEXTILES IN FASHION
CHAPTER TWO: MATERIALS
CHAPTER THREE: SURFACE DESIGN
CHAPTER FOUR: CONCEPTUALIZING THE COLLECTION
CHAPTER FIVE: SOURCING YOUR FABRIC
CHAPTER SIX: TEXTILES AND THE COLLECTION
SOURCING INTERVIEWS
APPENDIX

3 Not all patterns are printed onto fabric but may be created in the construction stage. A mad mix of plaids by Vivienne Westwood.

4 Resist and other hand dye techniques, by Giovanna Quercy.

Important aspects of pattern to be aware of when creating a custom print are original element or block, scale, and symmetry. All patterns are created by the structural repetition of a single **element** or **pattern block**. A pattern block is the smallest section of non-repetitive imagery in a pattern. **Scale** is the size of the element or block within the repeat. Some seasons oversized prints will be in fashion, other seasons miniaturized patterns will be in. **Symmetry** refers to the way the repetition of an element or pattern block is structured. If an element is symmetrical, like a single dot, then it can only be repeated in a straight grid (creating a cross pattern) or **offset** by degrees (creating an angled pattern). If an element is asymmetrical the repeat can **mirror** (reflect in opposite), **rotate** (turn 90 degrees around a central point), or **kaleidoscope** (radiate around an offset point). By employing the previous techniques in various combinations, 17 different types of pattern symmetry can be achieved. When working with a pattern block, it is important to know that the elements found on opposite edges (left to right and top to bottom) must be matched to create a **seamless repeat**. Pattern blocks are laid out in either straight or offset grid. **CAD** programs can be purchased that will automate various repeat pattern designs from a single element or make the creation of seamless repeat much easier.

Print processes

There are numerous methods for applying print and pattern to textiles. These range from simple hand techniques, which require minimal supplies, to full-scale mechanized processes capable of turning out many yards a minute. When sourcing already printed fabrics the process may not matter as much as how the fabric fits into the designer's budget and vision. Sometimes a designer's line has special parameters such as environmental awareness or exclusivity. In cases such as these certain processes may appeal to a designer's customer base and can be referenced for marketing. When creating custom fabrics for a collection the technique a designer chooses to employ will be affected by ability, funding, production needs and target market. How these factors affect surface design choice is discussed in Chapter 4. Either way it is important that print choice remains design led.

Traditional methods of fabric printing are done by hand. While labour intensive, these methods result in outstandingly beautiful textiles. In recent years much attention has been given to preserving traditional arts and hand-processed textiles can add significant value to the end product. It is also easier to find environmental answers when controlling the process. When creating a custom textile it is advisable to always make a sample using the exact fabric, mediums and methods to be used for production. This sample should be laundered according to label recommendation on the final garment to make sure the print will hold up. It is advisable to always wash a textile prior to printing to remove any sizing or finishing agents that might affect adherence of printing medium to fabric.

89

DECORATIVE DYE EFFECTS
PRINT AND PATTERN
EMBROIDERY
THREE-DIMENSIONAL SURFACE TECHNIQUES
DESIGNER SPOTLIGHT – ANNA SUI

5

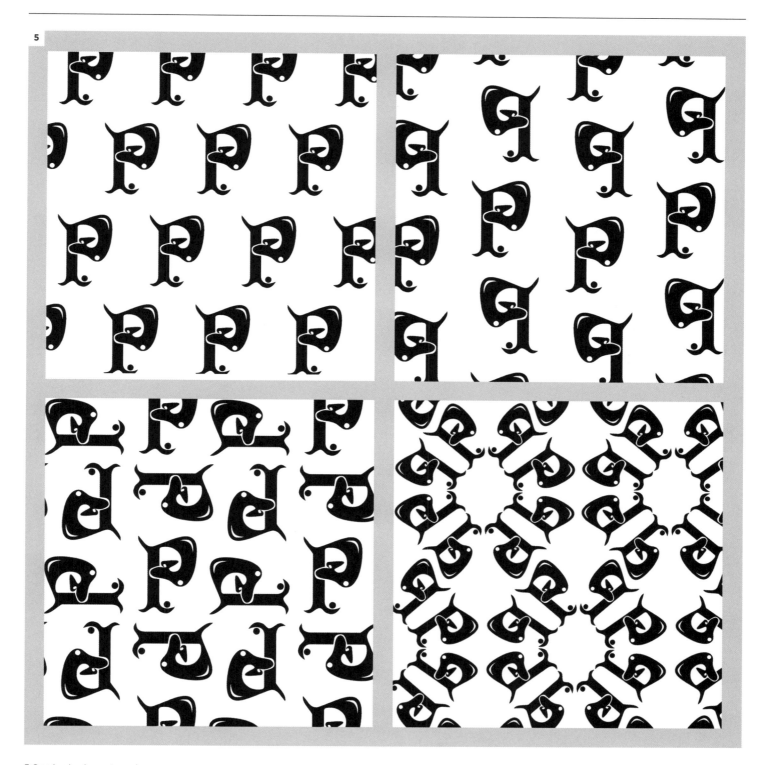

5 One basic element can be repeated utilizing different symmetry combinations to create various patterns.

Top left: Horizontal offset.
Top right: Mirror plus vertical offset.
Bottom left: Grid plus rotation.
Bottom right: Kaleidoscope plus horizontal offset.

**SOURCING AND SELECTING
TEXTILES FOR FASHION**

CHAPTER ONE: THE ROLE OF TEXTILES IN FASHION
CHAPTER TWO: MATERIALS
CHAPTER THREE: SURFACE DESIGN
CHAPTER FOUR: CONCEPTUALIZING THE COLLECTION
CHAPTER FIVE: SOURCING YOUR FABRIC
CHAPTER SIX: TEXTILES AND THE COLLECTION
SOURCING INTERVIEWS
APPENDIX

6

6 1939 conversational print on cotton dress by Elsa Schiaparelli (Italian, 1890–1973).

7 A selection of custom-designed fabrics by Eye Dazzler Design Studio Brooklyn, NY.

The easiest and hardest method of customizing fabric is hand painting. It is the easiest because few tools are needed, and the hardest because it will take considerable talent and time to produce any significant amount of yardage. Hand painting is best applied in a spot design, however it is important to remember there will be differences garment to garment when free handing an image. Block printing is a process of stamping an image in a regular pattern onto fabric. Traditionally carved blocks of wood dipped in ink were used. Any object that will hold up to repetitive stamping can be used. Another method of block printing is to apply ink to a carved block or textured surface, lay the textile face down onto the inked surface and apply even pressure to transfer the ink to the surface of the cloth. The most versatile studio method is screen printing. Screen printing is the process of using a squeegee to force ink through a partially blocked fabric screen onto a surface material. The unblocked areas of the screen allow the ink through to make an impression. Methods for blocking the screen are stencil, hand-painted screen filler or light sensitive photo emulsion that allows for highly detailed images. Screen printing can be used for spot or repeat printing. Large-scale screens can be made for printing many yards of fabric at once. Screen printing presses can be purchased that allow for exact registration of multicolour images.

Most pre-printed fabrics are created by massive rotary printing machines. Roller printing is a fairly new process – just a couple of centuries old. Roller machines hold a series of cylinders the width of the fabric. The cylinders are each engraved, etched or machine indented with one colour's part of the image to be printed. As the fabric passes by each cylinder the ink held in the engraved areas is transferred to the fabric. The mechanization of cylinders allow for continuous and seamless printing of multicolour images at 45.72 to 91.44 m (50 to 100 yd) per minute. Automated screen printing is also used for large runs of yardage. Flatbed screen printing machines use a series of screens with automated squeegees to print multicolour images. New machines can print 1,097.3 m (1,200 yd) per hour with a 91.44 cm (36 in) design repeat. Rotary screen printing combines the cylinder of roller machines with the screening method. Inks are forced through perforated cylinders onto fabric at 3,200.4 m (3,500 yd) per hour. These methods are costly and require high minimums, taking custom printed yardage out of reach of many designers. Recent advancements in the process of digital fabric printing have opened up fast, easy, multicolour textile printing to designers of all levels.

7

**SOURCING AND SELECTING
TEXTILES FOR FASHION**

CHAPTER ONE: THE ROLE OF TEXTILES IN FASHION
CHAPTER TWO: MATERIALS
CHAPTER THREE: SURFACE DESIGN
CHAPTER FOUR: CONCEPTUALIZING THE COLLECTION
CHAPTER FIVE: SOURCING YOUR FABRIC
CHAPTER SIX: TEXTILES AND THE COLLECTION
SOURCING INTERVIEWS
APPENDIX

92

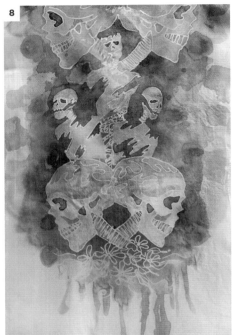

10 The ability to print registered multicolour designs in large amounts made patterned textiles available to all market levels. Child's cotton dress roller printed, 1820. Image © Vintage Textile.

11 Carved block used for traditional Indian repeat block printing. Design Cheryl Kolander.

8 Hand-painting gives freedom of expression but it can be hard to stay consistent during production. Hand-painted scarf by Shaelyn Zhu ©2011 undergraduate work

9 Non-registered multicolour screen prints are possible with very basic equipment. Ecofriendly screen printed T-shirt by THREE Erin Cadigan.

93

DECORATIVE DYE EFFECTS
PRINT AND PATTERN
EMBROIDERY
THREE-DIMENSIONAL SURFACE TECHNIQUES
DESIGNER SPOTLIGHT – ANNA SUI

12 Multicolour screen printed yardage is possible by hand or machine. Award-winning hand-printed fabric by Liora Rimoch.

SOURCING AND SELECTING
TEXTILES FOR FASHION

CHAPTER ONE: THE ROLE OF TEXTILES IN FASHION
CHAPTER TWO: MATERIALS
CHAPTER THREE: SURFACE DESIGN
CHAPTER FOUR: CONCEPTUALIZING THE COLLECTION
CHAPTER FIVE: SOURCING YOUR FABRIC
CHAPTER SIX: TEXTILES AND THE COLLECTION
SOURCING INTERVIEWS
APPENDIX

94

PRINTING TRUE BLACK

When generating an image using true black it is best to not use a CAD program's default black. Rather, go into the program's colour picker and manually set the ink commands to cyan=50%, magenta=40%, yellow=40% and black=100% to achieve the blackest black from an inkjet printer.

Digital printing

Digital textile printing differs from traditional and industrial methods in a number of ways. Fundamental skills and training required for pattern and print creation are much lower. Anyone with an artistic bent can take a short course in one of many different CAD programs available. These programs range from photograph manipulation and art creation to automatically generating complex repeat prints from very basic elements. No further skill is required to transfer images generated directly to textile. No colour separation is needed for the artwork as there are no screens or cylinders to make. Colours are not applied one at a time by direct contact as with other processes. Instead digital printers use a series of nozzles or heads to spray inks onto the fabric from above. Artwork is passed directly from the computer to the printer electronically, eliminating the need for any tangible art supplies or printing tools. Unlike other processes digital printing is suited to any amount of fabric, from sample to large production runs. However, the cost is often more expensive than other methods.

The inks used are cyan (turquoise blue), magenta (rubella pink), yellow and black. By combining these four inks in various amounts an inkjet printer can produce 256 shades of each of the four colours, a seemingly full gamut. However, it can be difficult to produce some colours such as bright orange or deep violet. Printers with an extra two heads, running CcMmYK rather than CMYK, can considerably expand the gamut. Regardless, digital printers far exceed colour capabilities of any other print method. Inkjet images are created from a series of tiny ink droplets; this is referred to as **DPI** (dots per inch). Digital textile printers can now be found that print at a resolution of 1440 dpi but any printer that operates at over 300 dpi will be able to reproduce highly complex photorealistic images.

There are four types of inks used in digital printing, each with its advantages and disadvantages. **Reactive inks** produce bright colours with good light and wash fastness. Fabrics need to be pre-treated with a bonding agent and post treated with steaming and washing. These inks are good for natural fibres such as cotton, silk and hemp. **Acid inks** also produce bright colour but have excellent colour fastness. These inks are ideal for swimwear, sportswear and leather goods. A pre-treatment is needed as well as post steaming and washing. **Disperse inks** (the first digital textile dyes) are used only for polyester or poly-blends. The images produced are not as bright as reactive or acid dyes but have excellent colour fastness. Low-energy disperse inks can be printed onto paper and then transferred to fabric through a heat set process called **dye sublimation**. High-energy disperse inks are used for direct-to-fabric applications then heat set. **Pigmented inks** can be used across a wide variety of fabric types. However, since they are applied in a dry application, the pigments sit on top of the fibres. As pigments build to darker shades the hand of the fabric is affected. Pigment inks have excellent light fastness and good wash fastness in lighter colour ranges. As colours get darker, wash fastness is not as good. These inks are very simple to use. Fabrics require no pre-treatment and only post-UV curing.

95

DECORATIVE DYE EFFECTS
PRINT AND PATTERN
EMBROIDERY
THREE-DIMENSIONAL SURFACE TECHNIQUES
DESIGNER SPOTLIGHT – ANNA SUI

13

14

13 & 14 Photorealistic digital placement prints by Greek designer Mary Katrantzou A/W 2012.

SOURCING AND SELECTING
TEXTILES FOR FASHION

CHAPTER ONE: THE ROLE OF TEXTILES IN FASHION
CHAPTER TWO: MATERIALS
CHAPTER THREE: SURFACE DESIGN
CHAPTER FOUR: CONCEPTUALIZING THE COLLECTION
CHAPTER FIVE: SOURCING YOUR FABRIC
CHAPTER SIX: TEXTILES AND THE COLLECTION
SOURCING INTERVIEWS
APPENDIX

96

1 Hand-embroidered ecofriendly dress design based on the Mayan creation story. Courtesy Erin Cadigan 2009.

2 Wild flowers, copied from a Dutch still life are embroidered using narrow satin ribbon onto a black net gown. Valentino, Fall/Winter 2013.

EMBROIDERY

Embroidery is the art of creating surface design through ornate needlework. Raised designs are threaded onto the surface of a fabric in decorative patterns created by precise and repetitive stitches. Contrasting, multicolour or metallic threads are used to help the work stand out on the background textile. Some techniques use threads matched to fabric or embroidery may be added to a garment or textile before dyeing.

Prior to the widespread availability of printed textiles, embroidery was the most important means of decorating cloth. Most women had some skill in it and wealthy homes employed their own embroidery artisans. The work was done by hand and multiple styles were developed from a few basic techniques. In today's market affordable hand embroidery is often sourced from countries where these skills are still prevalent. Most production embroidery is done by machine.

Stitches

Hand-done embroidery relies on one needle and one thread. It is all about where and how the thread is placed. **Line stitches** are common in most forms of embroidery. They are used to draw, outline or fill. Line stitches are simple, like the basic in-and-out **running stitch** or complex, like **couching** in which the 'line' is created by a yarn held in place by small thread stitches. **Chain stitching** is formed by linking one looped stitch through the previous stitch. **Backstitch** and **split stitch** are techniques in which the thread is pierced by the next stitch. **Detached stitches** are stitch elements that stand alone. **Detached chain** is a loop of thread caught by a small anchoring stitch, good for creating flower petals. **Fly stitch** uses an anchoring stitch to create a 'V' shape. **French** (or double looped) **knots** can be used singularly or to create a textured fill. **Cross stitch** is formed by repetitive and precise 'X' stitches. **Satin stitches** are closely placed side by side to create a smooth raised design. While it takes patience and skill to master embroidery, it is an easy art form to pick up. Materials are inexpensive and stitches can be learned through books.

2

SOURCING AND SELECTING
TEXTILES FOR FASHION

CHAPTER ONE: THE ROLE OF TEXTILES IN FASHION
CHAPTER TWO: MATERIALS
CHAPTER THREE: SURFACE DESIGN
CHAPTER FOUR: CONCEPTUALIZING THE COLLECTION
CHAPTER FIVE: SOURCING YOUR FABRIC
CHAPTER SIX: TEXTILES AND THE COLLECTION
SOURCING INTERVIEWS
APPENDIX

98

3

3 All-over machine embroidered
T-shirt, embroidered by a lace-
making machine. Patrik Ervell
S/S 2006.

Styles

Free embroidery is a style in which the designs and stitches are not based on the weave of the underlying fabric. Traditional embroidered motifs from China and Japan use free-style satin stitches to create elaborate figurative designs. **Crewel** embroidery is the use of multicoloured, heavy wool threads over the top of hand-drawn designs. Crewel work relies mainly on line stitching. **Redwork** (bluework) is an original grassroots embroidery technique from the turn of the century when penny patterns were sold on muslin squares and stitched over with one colour thread. Varied stitch styles were used.

Counted thread embroidery is done on any type of even weave fabric where the warp and weft threads produce an obvious repetitive pattern. Embroiderers count the fabric threads to help lay out the embroidery design. Many traditional techniques rely on this method. **Assisi** style works in the negative. Embroidery fills create a background allowing the fabric to be seen in the decorative motif. **Blackwork**, originally twisted black thread on white backing, depicts geometric or floral patterns made up of regimented stitches that describe tonal values. Blackwork no longer refers to the colour combination but the style of the work. **Hardanger** (also known as **whitework**) uses white on white, combining counted thread techniques with drawn work. **Drawn work** employs a technique of removing weft or warp threads from the base. Embroidery stitches are used to bundle the remaining threads into open work patterns. Other counted thread styles are **cross stitch** and **needlepoint**.

Cutwork utilizes various embroidery stitch techniques to outline a pattern in which the 'fill' is cut from the base fabric. Eyelet fabrics and trims are a good example of this technique. **Machine embroidery** is the most widely employed technique in contemporary fashion. Aside from a few high-end artisan embroidery houses, most of the embroidery work in the United States and Europe is machine-made. The **Schiffli machine** is the most popular production embroidery machine, operating up to 1,000 needles it is capable of reproducing almost all hand-stitch methods. A Schiffli can produce embroideries from several inches to several yards wide.

DECORATIVE DYE EFFECTS
PRINT AND PATTERN
EMBROIDERY
THREE-DIMENSIONAL SURFACE TECHNIQUES
DESIGNER SPOTLIGHT – ANNA SUI

4

4 Whitework is the embroidery of a single colour, typically matching that of the base canvas, where design and skill is defined primarily by texture.

SOURCING AND SELECTING
TEXTILES FOR FASHION

CHAPTER ONE: THE ROLE OF TEXTILES IN FASHION
CHAPTER TWO: MATERIALS
CHAPTER THREE: SURFACE DESIGN
CHAPTER FOUR: CONCEPTUALIZING THE COLLECTION
CHAPTER FIVE: SOURCING YOUR FABRIC
CHAPTER SIX: TEXTILES AND THE COLLECTION
SOURCING INTERVIEWS
APPENDIX

1 Smocking is used on the sleeves, waistline and neckline of this dress from Valentino's Spring/Summer 2012 collection.

THREE-DIMENSIONAL SURFACE TECHNIQUES

Surface design can rise above the two-dimensional surface of the textile through either fabric manipulation or three-dimensional embellishment. Though these two surface techniques may be worked onto textile yardage often they are added to cut pattern pieces before garment construction or to the finished garment. The three-dimensional quality of these art forms adds movement and drama to a fashion silhouette.

Fabric manipulation can be used to create structure and form in a garment or to add a decorative element. Often these techniques do both at once. Both texture and pattern are achieved through various sewing, pressing, steaming and cutting methods. Fabric manipulation may be additive or subtractive. Embellishment is an additive art form. Three-dimensional objects are fixed to the surface of a textile with thread, adhesives or specially made housings. Embellishment objects can be functional, decorative or both.

Fabric manipulation

Fabric manipulation is the art of reshaping the surface of a textile through various structural and decorative techniques. Fabric manipulation can be said to have been part of clothing design from the start of wearable fabric creation. The draping techniques of the ancients used fabric manipulation to decoratively restructure a square of cloth to the human form. Manipulation techniques range from loosely binding and gathering fabric to heat setting semi-rigid forms into a textile.

Draping, gathering and smocking are soft-gather techniques that are used both structurally and decoratively. **Draping** takes place on a fit model or dress form. It is the method of twisting, cutting, gathering and binding fabric to sculpturally design a garment. **Gathering** is used to create extra fullness on a garment. Soft folds of fabric are pulled together along a loosely stitched thread or on a machine with a gathering foot and secured with a stay stitch. The size of the gathers depends on the original stitch spacing. Gathers are mainly found on apparel at joint areas such as the waist, shoulder or wrist. Narrow strips of fabric may be gathered to create **ruffles**. **Smocking** is the method of controlling fullness in a garment by shirring together small vertical rows of gathers. Traditionally done by hand using embroidery techniques, it is most often accomplished today with elastic threads sewn by machine.

101

DECORATIVE DYE EFFECTS
PRINT AND PATTERN
EMBROIDERY
THREE-DIMENSIONAL SURFACE TECHNIQUES
DESIGNER SPOTLIGHT – ANNA SUI

2

2 Crazy-patchwork dress, Jasper Conran Spring/ Summer 2013.

SOURCING AND SELECTING
TEXTILES FOR FASHION

CHAPTER ONE: THE ROLE OF TEXTILES IN FASHION
CHAPTER TWO: MATERIALS
CHAPTER THREE: SURFACE DESIGN
CHAPTER FOUR: CONCEPTUALIZING THE COLLECTION
CHAPTER FIVE: SOURCING YOUR FABRIC
CHAPTER SIX: TEXTILES AND THE COLLECTION
SOURCING INTERVIEWS
APPENDIX

102

3

3 Minipleated suit. Alexander
McQueen RTW S/S 2012.

Pleats and tucks are precisely planned-out gathers that have been secured to form a more rigid application. **Pleats** are sharp-edged vertical folds of fabric. **Knife pleats** are single folds all facing the same direction. **Box pleats** have double folds that face away from each other. **Inverted pleats** are two folds that face each other and are set close. **Minipleats** are very narrow, multiple heat-pressed pleats used to create texture and form. **Tucks** are narrow folds secured fully or partially along their length by stitching. Tucks may be set vertically, horizontally or diagonally on a garment. **Pintucks** are extremely narrow tucks seen on tuxedo shirts and children's clothing.

Quilting, patchwork and shibori are decorative techniques. **Quilting** uses stitching to decoratively catch a three-dimensional filler between two sheets of fabric. Continuously even **batting** is most often used allowing any design to be stitched on the face fabric but sometimes rope or another object is used to create distinct shapes. Certain fillers, like down, may be used to make quilting a functional aspect of outerwear design. **Patchwork** is stitching multiple scraps of fabric to create one textile. Specifically shaped scraps may be used to create distinct patterns or random organic shapes may be used in **crazy quilt** technique. At times quilting is added to patchwork to create texture. **Shibori** is the ancient Japanese art of binding and shaping textile with thread, and heat. Shibori can be used to create pattern with the addition of dye but structural shibori uses the technique to imprint a lasting texture into the textile. Any type of fabric can be used with permanent stitch, binding or knotting techniques. Heat sensitive textiles like silk or polyester must be used when creating permanent textures by restraining areas of the textile, steaming or heat pressing and then releasing the restraints.

Subtractive manipulation methods remove some fibres of the textile to create texture and pattern. **Cutwork** and **slashing** are traditional hand techniques generally used in conjunction with embroidery. Purposeful holes and slits in the fabric are secured with stitching so unintended ripping does not occur. **Laser cutting** is a modern version of these techniques. Heat generated laser beams are used to cut elaborate designs in a variety of materials. The heat of the laser fuses the edges of heat sensitive textiles but other fabrics may require stay stitching to prevent tearing. Leather and suede hold up well to laser cutting. **Distressing** is a fairly new manipulation technique. It is seen often in the denim and contemporary markets. Distressing is the act of cutting, tearing, ripping or wearing away the fibres of a fabric to create texture.

103

DECORATIVE DYE EFFECTS
PRINT AND PATTERN
EMBROIDERY
THREE-DIMENSIONAL SURFACE TECHNIQUES
DESIGNER SPOTLIGHT – ANNA SUI

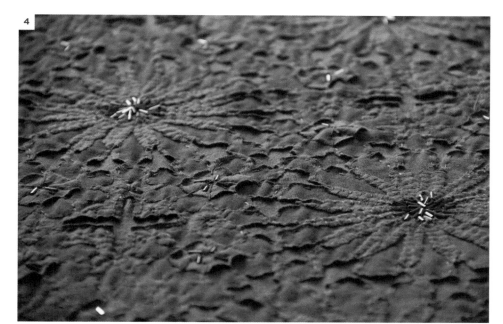

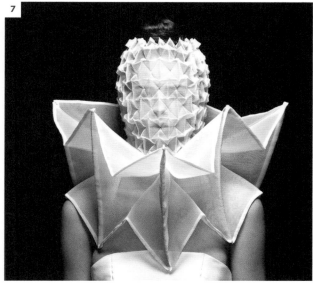

4 Hand-quilted jersey wrap. Adorned with delicate glass beading, all-over stencilling and intricate embroidery. Alabama Chanin 2012.

5 Distressed jersey knit dress by Brian Nussbaum.

6 The warrior vest is constructed with laser cut lambskin and embossed leather with brass rivets, coque feathers and leather fringe. Kelly Horrigan Handmade 2011.

7 Heat set shibori technique. Harrison Johnson.

**SOURCING AND SELECTING
TEXTILES FOR FASHION**

CHAPTER ONE: THE ROLE OF TEXTILES IN FASHION
CHAPTER TWO: MATERIALS
CHAPTER THREE: SURFACE DESIGN
CHAPTER FOUR: CONCEPTUALIZING THE COLLECTION
CHAPTER FIVE: SOURCING YOUR FABRIC
CHAPTER SIX: TEXTILES AND THE COLLECTION
SOURCING INTERVIEWS
APPENDIX

104

8

8 Knit Foley and Christina linen sweater with braid and tassel trims.

Embellishment

Embellishment is the addition of decorative three-dimensional objects to a textile surface. Traditionally, many cultures used meaningful objects to embellish the garments of significant people in their communities. Echoes of this can still be seen in modern-day military uniforms that sport braids, embroidered patches and brass buttons. Embellishments are also often used to accentuate the importance of an event simply because of the added expense to a garment.

When a designer desires an all-over embellished effect it is advisable to source a pre-embellished textile. Any hand-applied continuous embellishment will be cost prohibitive and will make economic sense only in the most high-end of collections.

Beading works for both casual and evening wear depending on the material the bead is made from. Beads are attached in patterns onto the surface of a textile by stitching. Larger beads can have fabric passed through their centres. You may see this on the straps of a sundress. **Sequins** are often used together with beads in evening wear applications. Sequins are small flat shapes of reflective material that are stitched onto a fabric. Larger **piallette sequins** are caught with thread and left to hang off the surface. Fully sequined fabrics and trims are easy to source. **Appliqué** is often mistaken for patchwork. Unlike patchwork, which attaches the edges of fabric shapes to each other, appliqué is the method of stitching those shapes on top of an existing textile. Rosettes, ruffles or any three-dimensional fabric object can be used, as well as flat shapes.

Many contemporary embellishments are attached to a textile through methods other then sewing. Flat backed **crystals**, metal look **'nailheads'** and **pyramid studs** can be inexpensively adhered to a textile surface with strong adhesives. In upscale fashion, quality versions of these items may be secured with a metal housing that pushes through the back of a fabric and entraps the bead. Some of these embellishments have self-adhering bendable points that can be pushed through fabric. **Metal spikes** can also be attached by a screw from the backside of the fabric. **Grommets, snaps, buttons** and **zippers** are all used as garment closures but in recent years have been trending as decorative embellishments for surface design.

Fringe can be made from any material that can be attached to a fabric in dangling strands. It can be applied in an all-over technique or as a trim. **Feathers, chains, braiding** and **tassels** are all readily available for purchase online or at any trim store. While these items may be made by hand, it is so easy to find a trim to match any desired style that not many designers bother with time consuming handmade trims.

105

DECORATIVE DYE EFFECTS
PRINT AND PATTERN
EMBROIDERY
THREE-DIMENSIONAL SURFACE TECHNIQUES
DESIGNER SPOTLIGHT – ANNA SUI

9

10

9 Evening cocktail blouse with sequin and beaded motif based on a celestial theme. By surreal designer Elsa Schiaparelli (Italian, 1890–1973).

10 Feather and tooled leather trim added to vintage wool overcoat. Professor Kelly Horrigan 2011.

SOURCING AND SELECTING
TEXTILES FOR FASHION

**DESIGNER
SPOTLIGHT**
ANNA SUI

106

Anna Sui's ready-to-wear collection is designed around patterned textiles. Each season her collection is a riot of contrasting and coordinating printed fabrics. She is a master at the use of colour and scale within surface treatment, and balance and proportion in construction methods to present a unified collection, even though each garment contains multiple prints, patterned textiles and/or surface treatments.

DISCUSSION QUESTIONS

1

Anna Sui is known for using multiple patterns and embellishments in each collection. What are some of the design elements she employs to give an overall unified look to each collection?

2

In your designs do you find the use of print and pattern enhances or distracts from the overall design concept? Why?

3

Do you think Anna Sui's work would stand out as much if she did not incorporate as many patterned textiles into each collection?

4

Though each collection uses very different patterns, Anna Sui still has an overall textile signature. How do you think she has managed to do that?

A fun mix of colour, print and texture. Anna Sui A/W 2012.

CHAPTER FOUR

Conceptualizing the Collection

One of the most important aspects of delivering an amazing fashion product to your customer is the sourcing of your base materials. Once a designer has an idea of what textiles they want to create their collection with, they must know how to find the proper textile and where to purchase it from. There are many sources for fashion textiles. Finding the proper vendors will depend on the size of your company, the market level of your product and the type of textile you are looking for. A designer may find their sources changing with each seasonal collection or they may form a lasting relationship with a textile vendor. Most likely there will be a combination of both new and trusted sources as the business grows.

When designing for an already established brand a designer may be given a list of reliable vendors, specific textile properties and characteristics to look for and be less financially restricted in textile selection. An emerging designer will need to budget and source carefully, spending a considerable amount of time locating fabrics. Either way there will be a costing budget to make sure the selected fabric does not exceed the projected manufacturing cost, as this will affect both wholesale and eventual retail price. If a fabulous but expensive textile is found, a designer can simplify construction details to minimize cost or reduce the budget on a second textile as a truly fantastic fabric can carry a collection.

Quality is remembered long after the price is forgotten.
Gucci slogan

**SOURCING AND SELECTING
TEXTILES FOR FASHION**

CHAPTER ONE: THE ROLE OF TEXTILES IN FASHION
CHAPTER TWO: MATERIALS
CHAPTER THREE: SURFACE DESIGN
CHAPTER FOUR: CONCEPTUALIZING THE COLLECTION
CHAPTER FIVE: SOURCING YOUR FABRIC
CHAPTER SIX: TEXTILES AND THE COLLECTION
SOURCING INTERVIEWS
APPENDIX

110

> **Your art isn't for everyone. Once you understand this, you'll have an easier time finding the people who appreciate your work.**
> Alyson Stanfield

TARGET MARKET AND THE FASHION CALENDAR

Prior to establishing a fashion brand and its successive collections a designer should conduct research. In the beginning research for a successful fashion business is practical and analytical. In order to understand where their creative vision will fit in the fashion world and who will wear it, a designer should conduct a market analysis and base their decisions on this information. A designer will rarely be conducting this research on their own. As a student, classmates and professors will offer feedback and critiques. A professional designer may be part of a design team that exchanges ideas and may have a say in what type of line will be produced. In addition to a creative team it is wise for a professional designer to seek out business mentors or to hire a marketing team. The practical business decisions that must be established prior to design are: what type of merchandise will we produce, who will we sell it to and how many times a year will we offer new product? The information needed to make these choices can be found by consulting the fashion calendar and conducting a target market analysis.

The fashion calendar

Fashion is a cyclical business. Each calendar year fashion cycles through its own calendared schedule. All designers look first to the fashion calendar before creating a collection, because the type of season affects the range and type of garments produced. The main two selling seasons are spring/summer and autumn/winter. It is advisable to launch a new design collection for autumn/winter as the selling season is longer. This offers the designer more time to introduce themselves to the customer as well as extra time to work on their second collection. It is good to remember there will never be as much lead up preparation time as you have when working on your debut collection.

1

1 Stella McCartney strives to combine ethical fashion with a luxury market. Her RTW A/W 2012 collection featured embroidered textiles, embossed double crepes and stretch wools, selections based on season, ethics, trend and market.

SOURCING AND SELECTING
TEXTILES FOR FASHION

CHAPTER ONE: THE ROLE OF TEXTILES IN FASHION
CHAPTER TWO: MATERIALS
CHAPTER THREE: SURFACE DESIGN
CHAPTER FOUR: CONCEPTUALIZING THE COLLECTION
CHAPTER FIVE: SOURCING YOUR FABRIC
CHAPTER SIX: TEXTILES AND THE COLLECTION
SOURCING INTERVIEWS
APPENDIX

112

SLOW FASHION

There has been a recent movement in fashion in response to shortened lead and selling times resulting from the growing popularity of additional seasons. This movement is called slow fashion. Slow fashion designers will typically produce one collection a year. Some designers add or subtract a season specific item or two to an otherwise seasonless assortment. Others will create a standard range their brand is known for, only offering it in new textiles or new detailing year to year. Both ethical and environmental concerns have played a part in the development of this trend.

2

Due to the need for manufacturing lead times fashion collections are shown approximately six months ahead of the season in which they will be sold. Fashion weeks are held in major cities including New York, London and Paris. Buyers and press view a designer's collection during this time. Designers may present their collection in a runway show or at meetings in a showroom. Depending on reaction and orders an edited line may be put into production from the initial garment range offered. The textiles used to create the sample or runway collection must be available to meet production needs. In order to ensure this a designer may have to buy some hard-to-source fabrics ahead of time, based on predictions of what will sell, or confine their textile selection to fabrics they are certain will be available in any quantity for production.

In addition to the two main selling seasons, others have arisen in the modern fashion calendar that a designer may or may not design for. These additional seasons are haute couture, holiday/resort and pre-autumn. Some companies also split spring and summer into two distinct selling seasons. Whether or not these lesser seasons are a part of a designer's business plan will depend on target market, merchandise and market segmentation. Deciding to add a season to a fashion business is a serious decision as it will affect the bottom line both through man-hours and additional expenditure.

113

TARGET MARKET AND THE FASHION CALENDAR
INSPIRATION AND TREND
COLOUR IN FASHION
TEXTILE AND SILHOUETTE
SURFACE AND CONSTRUCTION CONSIDERATIONS
DESIGNER SPOTLIGHT – RODARTE

2 (opposite) Australian streetwear brand Ksubi knows its market so well it is able to offer seasonal styles in custom finishes and one-of-a-kind detailing. Seasonal pieces are modified through experimentation and specialist fabric treatments from bleaching, tie-dyeing, printing, embroidery, studding and shredding to ensure limited runs.

Target market

In order to succeed a business must understand its target customer. This is inordinately true in fashion as many people use clothing as a way to broadcast their identity to the world. Knowing exactly who this person is and what are their identifying characteristics will inform the selection of textiles, surface design treatments and the apparel line that is produced. In fashion this analysis starts with merchandise segmentation. **Merchandise segmentation** is broken into three categories: womenswear, menswear and children's wear. These categories are further broken down into market segmentation. How many different market levels there are depend on which of the three merchandise segments your product range falls into and whether you sell mainly to the United States or in Europe. There are 12 distinct womenswear markets in the US but only six in Europe. Womenswear market segments include haute couture, designer, contemporary and mass market. **Market segmentation** affects the costing of a fashion item including quality and affordability of textiles.

In addition to standard fashion segmentations it is a good idea to delve further into who your customer is with a target market analysis. When analysing the consumer base of your fashion brand what you want to end up with is a distinct picture of who this person is, what they look like, what they wear and their projected persona. In fashion there may be a disconnect between the person you design for and the person who actually buys. This happens when the image your line portrays is so inspirational that the buyer wants to literally buy that person's image.

Target market starts with **gender** and/or sexual orientation reflecting in menswear or womenswear, masculine or feminine styling. **Age** and **socio-economic status** will affect fabric selection, style of surface treatments, colour choice and silhouette. Generally manufacturing quality and design sophistication rise in tandem with both. **Lifestyle** and **physicality** of a customer will offer insight into technological requirements of textiles used and size range of the line. Stretch fabrics may be needed either for an active or plus size customer. **Environmental** factors such as weather and location may signify specialized items such as outerwear for northern climates or club wear for urban life. **Socio-cultural values** such as religious beliefs, political affiliation, environmental concerns and ethnicity may inform materials, silhouette and print pattern.

SOURCING AND SELECTING
TEXTILES FOR FASHION

CHAPTER ONE: THE ROLE OF TEXTILES IN FASHION
CHAPTER TWO: MATERIALS
CHAPTER THREE: SURFACE DESIGN
CHAPTER FOUR: CONCEPTUALIZING THE COLLECTION
CHAPTER FIVE: SOURCING YOUR FABRIC
CHAPTER SIX: TEXTILES AND THE COLLECTION
SOURCING INTERVIEWS
APPENDIX

114

INSPIRATION AND TREND

A designer does not design in a void. In today's fast paced and globally connected environment we are all constantly bombarded with information both visual and conceptual. There is no real way to unplug our minds from ingesting, processing and regurgitating all that we see and experience. As artists and designers we strive for originality and an individualized point of view. However as humans we connect to the world around us in unperceivable ways. Trends form out of these unperceived currents. These currents are the *collective consciousness.* This concept is used to explain how even the trend makers will often present concurrent collections influenced by the same inspiration. Where a collection falls in the life of a trend depends on how aware and astute the designer is at processing seemingly unconnected information.

Inspiration and trend can be directly translated into fabric selection. Sometimes the interpretation will be obvious and literal. For example, if sheer is trending a designer will add chiffon, organza, netting or clear vinyl into their fabric selection. Other times it may be more conceptual and figurative. A new and critically acclaimed movie or gallery show may inspire translation into colour, silhouette or print trends.

Inspiration

Once a brand concept has been established, a customer identified and season noted it is time for the design team to research inspiration. **Inspiration** can come from one source or many. Inspiration is all around us. It has become the job of the fashion industry to 'clothe the **zeitgeist**', or dress the spirit of the times. A designer does this by staying current and educated in more than just fashion. Art can inspire through music, film, paintings and theatre. Culture can inspire through tradition, politics and social interactions. Design can inspire through books, architecture, industrial design and interiors. Research must be conducted by experience. Travel, visit galleries, theatres and lectures, explore new music, read books, shop. Keep a constant awareness of the world around you.

The past can also be an inspiration for the present. Designers will often find inspiration in a vintage article of clothing or specific time period. Customers will often seek out fashion items that strike a chord of nostalgia. This tends to trend in 20-year cycles. The 1970s inspired the 90s, the 1980s the 2000s. A designer must be careful not to get too literal with the past or a collection may seem dated or costume.

115

TARGET MARKET AND THE FASHION CALENDAR
INSPIRATION AND TREND
COLOUR IN FASHION
TEXTILE AND SILHOUETTE
SURFACE AND CONSTRUCTION CONSIDERATIONS
DESIGNER SPOTLIGHT – RODARTE

1 Many collections start in the designer's sketchbook. Courtesy of Caroline Kaufman.

2 Concept boards can be pieced together from fashion references, textiles, editorial content and found objects. Aza Ziegler, Pratt Institute.

3 A collage of found images and textures will be used to inspire trend, silhouette, fabric selection and colour palette. Courtesy of Julianna Horner, undergraduate work ©2011.

**SOURCING AND SELECTING
TEXTILES FOR FASHION**

CHAPTER ONE: THE ROLE OF TEXTILES IN FASHION
CHAPTER TWO: MATERIALS
CHAPTER THREE: SURFACE DESIGN
CHAPTER FOUR: CONCEPTUALIZING THE COLLECTION
CHAPTER FIVE: SOURCING YOUR FABRIC
CHAPTER SIX: TEXTILES AND THE COLLECTION
SOURCING INTERVIEWS
APPENDIX

116

PRESENTATION BOARDS

Inspiration board – Initial and transitional in studio board or packet where design and marketing teams assemble and work the upcoming seasons inspirations and trends.

Mood board – Finalized concept board made of key elements from inspiration board used to solidify and illustrate inspiration, customer, market and colour story to viewer.

Story boards – Mood board plus fashion illustrations and CAD or hand-drawn flats line sheet used in a portfolio or market presentation to describe a collection.

It is advisable to constantly carry a sketchbook or notebook to record instances of inspiration when they strike. Reminders should be written, magazine clippings and fabric scraps pasted in and drawings recorded of daily inspiration. As time draws closer to the start of a new collection the design team should review and condense what is most inspiring for this season's fashion collection. At this point further research into the chosen inspiration should be conducted and an inspiration board assembled. An **inspiration board** can be a wall or board in a design studio, where images, drawings, fabrics and trims can be added and subtracted as the collection is worked. Inspiration should be kept visible to all designers working on a collection and referred back to constantly. Later on a finalized mood board and story boards can be made to help explain and present a collection to investors, the marketing team, press or buyers.

Trend

As explained in earlier chapters textile trends are at least two years ahead of fashion trends. Mills analyse information coming in from current purchase orders and reorders. Upon compiling the textures, hands, colours and prints that have sold best they project into the future, trying to predict where these trends will lead, if they have crested or if they are waning. All mills must have some sort of trend analysis department to stay current; major mills employ full-time trend forecasters. Textile forecasting is important because no matter what happens in the interim, the textiles, textures, prints and colours being manufactured now will be what is readily available to designers two or three years down the road.

Trend prediction plays a major role in fashion. Most professional designers, design teams and design schools subscribe to some form of professional trend forecasting. This may come from textile or trade fairs, or forecast packages, publications or websites. If there is no formal subscription they employ in-house or personal research into what is happening in the marketplace. Some design students believe that they will never follow or pay attention to trends as if to do so will somehow make them less of a creative designer. This is untrue and more importantly to look at design as simply an art form may leave the student designer without a professional life. Fashion design is a business; its history is business and conceiving fashion strictly as art is a recent development. One of the main objectives of any business is profit. In order to stay in business a designer must be aware that consumers are susceptible to trend. A successful fashion house will know if their customer base sets, rides or follows the current trends and design accordingly.

117

TARGET MARKET AND THE FASHION CALENDAR
INSPIRATION AND TREND
COLOUR IN FASHION
TEXTILE AND SILHOUETTE
SURFACE AND CONSTRUCTION CONSIDERATIONS
DESIGNER SPOTLIGHT – RODARTE

TYPES OF TREND

Fad – A fashion trend that starts, peaks and wanes in one season.

Trend – A colour, silhouette, surface treatment or style that starts with early adopters, hits the fashion conscious and eventually fades into the general population, lasts over several seasons.

Classic – Generally a colour or silhouette that forms, peaks and never really recedes from fashion, think black or trench coat.

Design protection

One thing to be aware of when looking to past or present art and design trends for inspiration is **design infringement**. This is when a designer crosses a line from being inspired by someone else's art to copying all or part verbatim. In the fashion world this is called a knock-off and it has become epidemic. Most of the problem has arisen from intentional design infringement by foreign factories looking to make a quick buck by producing fake luxury items that closely resemble the original and bear its branding label or **trademark**. However, all designers must take care not to unintentionally reproduce someone else's work too closely.

There are laws that offer some protection to a designers work. Due to the nature of the laws it can be hard to legally prove design infringement. Any serious designer must self regulate and be aware of the social and critical ramifications within the fashion world to design piracy. **Copyright** laws can safely protect textile design, print and pattern as these can be seen as strictly artistic work. Some designers choose to work with copyright images through licensing agreements with the image's owner. In a licensing deal a design firm will pay royalties or a percentage of profit to use a copyrighted image in their design. **Dress** (apparel) **design** is considered utilitarian and is not copyrightable unless artistic merit can be separated from functionality. **Trademark** laws protect a brand's identity and logo. In a recent addition to trademark law, trade dress can protect the overall appearance of a product including design. Some well-known companies will license their trademark as well (Reidelbach and Wilson, 2002).

4 Designers work with all collected information to assess where their line should fall within trending fashions. Courtesy Pratt Institute Fashion Department.

5 Stylesight.com is a well-known trend prediction site for fashion design.

**SOURCING AND SELECTING
TEXTILES FOR FASHION**

CHAPTER ONE: THE ROLE OF TEXTILES IN FASHION
CHAPTER TWO: MATERIALS
CHAPTER THREE: SURFACE DESIGN
CHAPTER FOUR: CONCEPTUALIZING THE COLLECTION
CHAPTER FIVE: SOURCING YOUR FABRIC
CHAPTER SIX: TEXTILES AND THE COLLECTION
SOURCING INTERVIEWS
APPENDIX

118

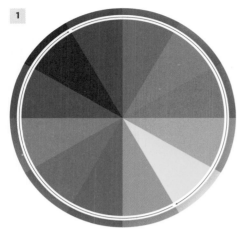

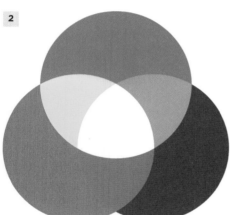

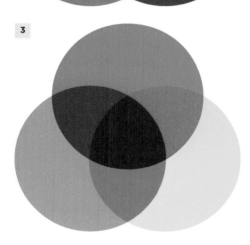

1 The colour wheel.

2 Additive colour theory mixes the primary colours of light: red, blue and green. These are the colours used by electronic screens to create all colour. This theory is not often utilized in fashion design.

3 These three colours with the addition of black are the dye colours used by digital and offset printers to create a full gamut of visible colour.

COLOUR IN FASHION

Colour elicits an immediate response in people. It is perhaps the most personal and emotive element within any designer collection. Colour in fashion cycles through both season and trends. Technological advances in pigments and dyes may impact the market as new colours become possible. Colour trends are affected by popular culture, economic climate and consumer values. How and why a designer chooses a colour palette will depend on their brand aesthetic, target market, seasonal inspiration and current trends. Depending on how fashion-forward its market segment is, a brand's designer may have more or less flexibility with colour trend. Choosing the colour palette for a design collection is serious business: it is one of the top reasons a consumer will buy or reject a product.

Colour theory

When working with colour it is important to understand some key concepts. **Colour** is created by the reflection of light wavelengths off a surface. A full **spectrum** of rays hit a surface, which absorbs some rays and bounces back others. It is the bounced-back rays that the human eye perceives as an object's colour. The visible light spectrum is red, orange, yellow, green, blue, indigo and violet. In design, these six colours (minus indigo) create the basic colour wheel. The primary colours of red, yellow and blue are mixed to create the secondary colours of green, orange and purple. An advanced colour wheel will continue to mix neighbouring colours creating tertiary (for example yellow-green), quaternary and beyond. These different **hues** may also be shown mixed with differing amounts of black and white to create a spectrum of **shades** and **tints** respectively. Mixing colours that are across the wheel from each other will create a variety of browns or greys. **Colour wheel** theory will be used when mixing fabric dyes, paints and screen printing inks.

The colour wheel can be used as a tool to show the conceptual relationship between colours. Neighbouring colours on the wheel are **analogous**. Colours set opposite on the wheel are **complementary**. **Split complementary colours** combine one colour plus the two immediate neighbours of its complement colour. Other colour theories may be created by superimposing an equilateral triangle (**triad**), **square** or rectangle (**tetradic**) shape over the colour wheel. These complex colour combinations all work best when one colour is dominant and the others are used in lesser degrees.

Colour may also be theorized in what is called additive and subtractive colour theory. **Additive colour** theory mixes the primary colours of light: red, blue and green and **subtractive colour** theory uses the secondary colours produced in the additive colour wheel: magenta, yellow and cyan. These three colours, with the addition of black, are used by digital and offset printers to create a full gamut of visible colour.

119

TARGET MARKET AND THE FASHION CALENDAR
INSPIRATION AND TREND
COLOUR IN FASHION
TEXTILE AND SILHOUETTE
SURFACE AND CONSTRUCTION CONSIDERATIONS
DESIGNER SPOTLIGHT – RODARTE

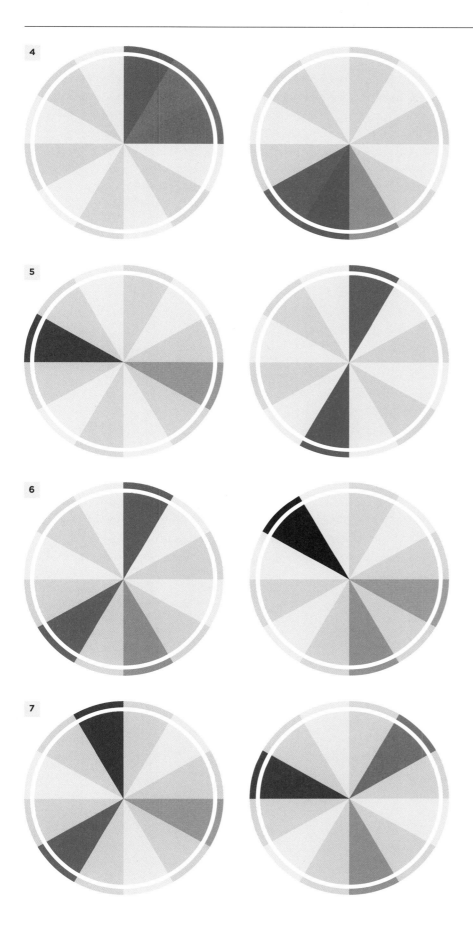

4 Analogous colours match well and create a consistent and harmonious collection. Use one to dominate, one to support and one to accent.

5 Complementary colours must be used carefully. Certain combinations can be jarring but they may also create a dynamic collection.

6 Split complementaries are often a better solution as they have the same drama but less visual tension.

7 Triads are formed of three equally spaced colours on the wheel. One colour should dominate and the other two be used as accents.

SOURCING AND SELECTING
TEXTILES FOR FASHION

CHAPTER ONE: THE ROLE OF TEXTILES IN FASHION
CHAPTER TWO: MATERIALS
CHAPTER THREE: SURFACE DESIGN
CHAPTER FOUR: CONCEPTUALIZING THE COLLECTION
CHAPTER FIVE: SOURCING YOUR FABRIC
CHAPTER SIX: TEXTILES AND THE COLLECTION
SOURCING INTERVIEWS
APPENDIX

120

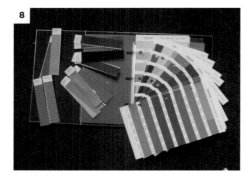

8 Pantone is a world leader in colour research and trend. They put out various standardized colour guides for dyes, paints and inks used by many different industries. This allows accurate colour conversations to occur between non-local parties. By utilizing these systems a designer in New York can ask a factory in Asia to dye a textile Pantone 19-4056 and receive back the exact trend colour, Olympian Blue, they requested.

9 A fashion design using tertiary complements of blue-green and red-orange. China Bones by Lindsay Jones S/S 2011.

10 Silhouettes will be offered in various coordinating colours and prints to extend a collection. Line sheet courtesy of Arianna Elmy, undergraduate work ©2011.

Colour and textile

Once an inspiration for the collection has been decided upon, a designer will put together a coordinating **colour story** based on the inspiration, along with market research and trend. A colour story or palette is a selected grouping of colours. These colours will form the basis of textile selection for a collection. A designer may apply basic colour theories to enhance the harmony or drama planned for a range of garments. By choosing to use just one colour a designer may shift design focus to fabric textures, or garment construction methods and silhouette. When colour stories move into actual fabric selection other textile design elements will create complexity. Textile texture, print and pattern all complicate the colour story. When textiles with any of these elements are chosen in the same colour palette as a season's solid fabrics they are called **coordinates**. Often mills or textile designers will create a range of coordinates to **upsell** their fabric selection to a designer. In the same way a designer can offer interest within their collection and ensure added sales by using coordinate textiles within their seasonal line.

Colour is applied to textile through the various dye and print methods discussed in Chapter 3. Depending on the fibre content, construction method, dyestuff and print medium, colour can morph or alter slightly when applied to a textile. Colour names may be more universal than specific. Even what may be thought of as a standard colour name, such as black, will have hue variations across materials, not only between different companies but also within a selected company's product range. Therefore a designer must take care to always swatch selected fabrics and compare and contrast actual swatches with other textile options. If sourcing non-locally, leave time to receive a company's colour card or fabric samples prior to ordering. When sourcing from a local store or trade fair move a fabric into a different light source if possible, as many colours shift under differing types of light. When creating custom fabrics always sample dye and print on exact fabric using the same methods and mediums intended for production. These extra efforts may save some unfortunate colour mishaps down the road.

121

TARGET MARKET AND THE FASHION CALENDAR
INSPIRATION AND TREND
COLOUR IN FASHION
TEXTILE AND SILHOUETTE
SURFACE AND CONSTRUCTION CONSIDERATIONS
DESIGNER SPOTLIGHT – RODARTE

10

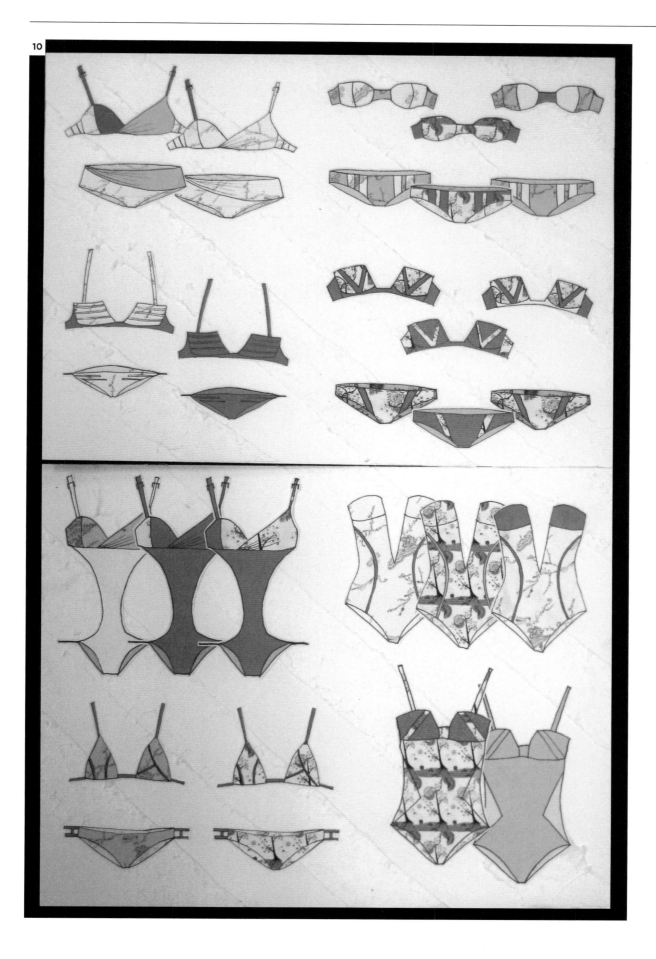

SOURCING AND SELECTING
TEXTILES FOR FASHION

CHAPTER ONE: THE ROLE OF TEXTILES IN FASHION
CHAPTER TWO: MATERIALS
CHAPTER THREE: SURFACE DESIGN
CHAPTER FOUR: CONCEPTUALIZING THE COLLECTION
CHAPTER FIVE: SOURCING YOUR FABRIC
CHAPTER SIX: TEXTILES AND THE COLLECTION
SOURCING INTERVIEWS
APPENDIX

122

1

1 Extra-wide shoulders and cocoon tailoring create a silhouette that is both boxy and oval on the Autumn 2012 runways. Jil Sander.

TEXTILE AND SILHOUETTE

Once a colour palette has been decided upon a designer will start to conceptualize the types of fabric needed to create their collection. Designers operate in one of two ways. They either start to sketch out design concepts, building and solidifying the line prior to sourcing textiles. Or they first go out searching for textiles that speak to the inspiration and colour story assembled, sourcing the textiles, print and pattern options available prior to starting the final design process. No matter which direction a designer takes, separating textile choice from garment design is impossible. A good designer must have a working knowledge of common textile properties and capabilities. Prior to either drawing out their designs or sourcing their textiles they must have some idea of both the intended textile selection and basic garment silhouettes planned for a collection in order to end up with a line range that matches season, inspiration and market.

Fashion silhouettes

The basic shape created by the outside edges of a garment when worn on the human form is called **silhouette**. These are categorized as six basic shapes. **Oval** contains soft, voluminous silhouettes that may gather at the top and bottom but billow out from the body. **Square** or boxy are more rigid structured garments. The **rectangle** is a basic shift, top or trouser that skims close to the human form without following it. **Inverted triangle** silhouettes may employ structural elements like shoulder pads to emphasis the narrowing to the waist or hip. On a bottom the inverted triangle can be seen in a carrot trouser with pleated hip and pegged ankle. **Triangle** is any silhouette that flows out from a narrow start. A structured A-line dress and full maxi-skirt are both examples. **Hourglass** follows the shape of a womanly body, narrowing at the waist but extending at the shoulder and hip. Common design foils like the capped sleeve, corset and peplum will emphasize the hourglass silhouette.

123

TARGET MARKET AND THE FASHION CALENDAR
INSPIRATION AND TREND
COLOUR IN FASHION
TEXTILE AND SILHOUETTE
SURFACE AND CONSTRUCTION CONSIDERATIONS
DESIGNER SPOTLIGHT – RODARTE

2 A triangle silhouette with exaggerated proportions by Junko Shimada. A/W 2012.

In addition to the six basic silhouettes many style and design categories are known in modern fashion as a **fashion silhouette**. These will often be the silhouettes referred to by trend forecasters and fashion press. One common recurring fashion silhouette trend for women is **menswear**. This silhouette is categorized by any garment shaping that replicates tailored men's clothing. Others may refer to a natural boho silhouette or a ruffled silhouette. These are efforts to either rename one of the six basic silhouettes in trendy terminology or to incorporate what is actually a principle of design into the discussion. The **principles of design** that may enhance or be applied to a silhouette are **rhythm, emphasis, gradation, repetition, contrast, balance, unity** and **proportion**. The first four will be added through surface design elements such as print, pattern, fabric manipulation or trims. The last four will be applied through fabric selection, cut and construction.

Textile to silhouette

For every silhouette and style there will be textiles that enhance or defeat the shape. This is why it is important to either have a deep understanding of common fashion textiles and their inherent properties or the ability to access a sizable swatch of your intended fabric. In actuality, no matter what your textile knowledge base is, it is always going to work out best for design to have a sample of the textile. Textile selection is a very tactile part of the design process. Whether designing to the selected fabric or matching textile to already designed silhouettes, how readily a textile drapes or holds structure, how far the bias will stretch, how the fabric reacts when gathered, pressed into a fold or heat steamed will be information that can only be judged through interaction with a physical sample. More importantly the true colour, texture and hand of a textile cannot be assumed though book knowledge or photo. Keep in mind that most customers will be drawn to the rack by colour or texture, and then touch the garment to judge its hand. Only after it passes these two tests will they pull it out to look at the silhouette and cut.

**SOURCING AND SELECTING
TEXTILES FOR FASHION**

CHAPTER ONE: THE ROLE OF TEXTILES IN FASHION
CHAPTER TWO: MATERIALS
CHAPTER THREE: SURFACE DESIGN
CHAPTER FOUR: CONCEPTUALIZING THE COLLECTION
CHAPTER FIVE: SOURCING YOUR FABRIC
CHAPTER SIX: TEXTILES AND THE COLLECTION
SOURCING INTERVIEWS
APPENDIX

124

3 Menswear-influenced fashion silhouettes. Kenzo A/W 2012.

4 (opposite page) Through the proper use of textile, drape and tailoring an oval silhouette becomes an hourglass. Max.Tan A/W 2010.

125

TARGET MARKET AND THE FASHION CALENDAR
INSPIRATION AND TREND
COLOUR IN FASHION
TEXTILE AND SILHOUETTE
SURFACE AND CONSTRUCTION CONSIDERATIONS
DESIGNER SPOTLIGHT – RODARTE

RELATING THE ELEMENTS OF DESIGN TO FASHION

The seven elements are the building blocks of all art and design. How can we translate them into fashion terminology?

Line – The human form, the path a draped textile will follow, fashion illustration

Colour – Colour story, seasonal colours, trend colours

Value – Accents through trim, contrast, black and white, neutrals

Shape – Basic six silhouettes, patterns and prints

Form – Sizing, length, structure, tailoring

Texture – Mood boards, textile surface, textile construction methods, surface embellishments

Space – Inspiration, fashion market, how a garment interacts with the world around it

4

If sourcing textiles by physical sample is not possible then researching fabric types and construction methods is the next best option. Never buy a fabric without some understanding of how it will behave. Medium-weight knit or woven fabrics are best for an oval silhouette. The textile should have a balance between drape and structure. Oval silhouette can also be forced through supporting a lightweight fabric, for example with tulle or cutting and tailoring a stiff textile into an exact egg silhouette. Square silhouettes are mostly achieved through tailoring a heavyweight woven fabric. However by using the arms as a structuring element a top or dress can be cut from a lighter fabric that hangs off the body in a forced square silhouette. The rectangle silhouette has the widest range of textile possibilities. A rectangle may be stiff like a classic denim jean, obvious like a classic broadcloth shift dress or soft and malleable like a silk jersey column-cut evening gown. A triangle silhouette most often is a medium to heavier weight woven combined with tailoring techniques to create a shape that gets wider as it falls towards the ground, essentially fighting gravity. A forced triangle can be created by bolstering a malleable knit or woven with a stiffer under fabric. The inverted triangle is really a silhouette built through the use of structuring elements like shoulder pads, interfacing or wire. A stiff medium-weight textile that can hold its shape but not weigh down the structure will be best. The hourglass is created through a combination of cut and construction techniques. Any weight woven textile can be used. Cut and sew knits may be used for a softer silhouette or straight to garment knits can be patterned to follow close to the human form.

SOURCING AND SELECTING TEXTILES FOR FASHION

CHAPTER ONE: THE ROLE OF TEXTILES IN FASHION
CHAPTER TWO: MATERIALS
CHAPTER THREE: SURFACE DESIGN
CHAPTER FOUR: CONCEPTUALIZING THE COLLECTION
CHAPTER FIVE: SOURCING YOUR FABRIC
CHAPTER SIX: TEXTILES AND THE COLLECTION
SOURCING INTERVIEWS
APPENDIX

126

SURFACE AND CONSTRUCTION CONSIDERATIONS

As a collection concept takes form, the design process moves from the abstract to the concrete and the macro to the micro. Once the design elements of colour and value, line, shape, texture, form and space have been decided upon it is time to apply the principles of design to a collection. In fashion we work the principles of design through surface design and construction details. Having a focused and well-edited cache of details is essential to a cohesive collection. If too many details are added to a collection it will look contrived and over designed. Any surface and construction plans must relate back to the inspiration and be able to work with both the selected textiles and silhouettes. As with other stages of design it is good to keep an eye on trends, as design details can make a fresh inspiration look dated or a basic silhouette look fashion forward. Target market and retail price points must always be kept in mind as surface and construction detailing costs can quickly add up, a balance must be kept between the perceived value these details add and cost of manufacturing. (A detailed look at costing can be found in Chapter 6, page 169.)

Surface design

Surface design methods are discussed in depth in Chapter 3. **Surface design** refers to any decorative design element added to the surface of a textile or garment. While colour elicits an emotive response, surface treatments are thought provoking. Because a surface design can incorporate texture, imagery and text there is a possibility of strong reference to time, place, people or things. The texture of an eyelet-embroidered sundress may nostalgically remind us of childhood summer days. A whimsical conversation print on a full skirt will reference the good time era of the American 1940s and 50s. A bold graphic and/or text may be used on a T-shirt to express a political or social view. Research and consideration should be used to make sure the chosen surface design matches the intended design statement.

1 Inspiration for print and texture can be taken from anywhere. Courtesy of Anne Lysonski, undergraduate work ©2011.

TARGET MARKET AND THE FASHION CALENDAR
INSPIRATION AND TREND
COLOUR IN FASHION
TEXTILE AND SILHOUETTE
SURFACE AND CONSTRUCTION CONSIDERATIONS
DESIGNER SPOTLIGHT – RODARTE

1

SOURCING AND SELECTING
TEXTILES FOR FASHION

CHAPTER ONE: THE ROLE OF TEXTILES IN FASHION
CHAPTER TWO: MATERIALS
CHAPTER THREE: SURFACE DESIGN
CHAPTER FOUR: CONCEPTUALIZING THE COLLECTION
CHAPTER FIVE: SOURCING YOUR FABRIC
CHAPTER SIX: TEXTILES AND THE COLLECTION
SOURCING INTERVIEWS
APPENDIX

128

2

Surface design follows its own trend trajectory. One season dip dye may be in and the next tie-dye methods. Or perhaps decorative dye techniques are out and all anyone wants is plaids. The question of whether or not to follow surface or market trends in your collection can often be ingeniously answered through manipulating methods. By manipulating the traditional method of delivery one can twist surface design and design statement in surprising ways. An intarsia knit anarchy sign on a prim sweater set becomes ironic; digitally printing a heavy cable knit texture on chiffon makes a summer-time fabric winter worthy. A fashion forward designer may see the dip dye trend as an opportunity to explore textile construction techniques that give a textural gradation to the fabric alluding to the dye gradations being used by other designers that season. When choosing a method keep in mind any implied messages it may make. If plaid is the trend it can be applied through textile construction (quality), printed (trendy), used in appliqué (children's wear) or beaded and embroidered onto a surface (fashion forward). A printed pattern motif can be used as an all-over continuous print (conservative) or one element of the motif can be sized up and strategically placed to add drama to a design (edgy).

The four principles of design most likely applied to a collection through surface design methods are rhythm, emphasis, gradation and repetition. **Rhythm** is repetitive pattern or texture. **Emphasis** is the use of one element or a combination of elements in a design to create a focal point. Trims, placement prints and embroideries are all used to emphasize areas of a garment. **Gradation** is the series of gradual changes in an element. We may use dye to create a gradation in colour or varying sizes of all-over sequins to create a gradation in texture. These gradations may be shown on one garment or slowly worked through the collection becoming obvious when seen together on the catwalk. **Repetition** uses an element repeatedly to create consistency and harmony. In a fashion garment this may be a surface treatment like pleating, in a collection this would be carrying the pleating method across several garments in the range.

2 If silhouette is balanced properly, over-the-top surface design can turn whimsical, sophisticated. Fringed, sequined, printed, woven, placed and all-over patterns on the runway at Jean-Charles de Castelbajac autumn 2011.

129

TARGET MARKET AND THE FASHION CALENDAR
INSPIRATION AND TREND
COLOUR IN FASHION
TEXTILE AND SILHOUETTE
SURFACE AND CONSTRUCTION CONSIDERATIONS
DESIGNER SPOTLIGHT – RODARTE

3 Textile choice can increase implied value but special construction considerations can also add cost. Vena Cava autumn 2011.

Construction

Some surface design methods are also construction techniques, but all surface design impacts construction. When choosing to add surface elements to a collection it is important to know whether or not they can technically be used both with the selected textile but also for the intended silhouette. Pintucks may be nearly impossible to achieve on a heavy double-knit fabric. If the design concept requires a relaxed rectangle silhouette choosing a heat-set shibori technique may be preferable over a permanent binding shibori that may stiffen the texture of the textile too much. Heavy beading or embroidery may distort a delicate fabric or weigh down a voluminous silhouette. It is best to add three-dimensional surface techniques to an already constructed garment to avoid bulk in construction or added cost for removal at seams to allow stitching. Care must also be taken when constructing a garment with a printed fabric. Pattern pieces must be carefully laid out on the textile to make sure obvious print elements, like stripes, match up at seams.

The four design principles that affect construction decisions are contrast, balance, proportion and unity. Contrast uses two opposite elements to create tension or highlight each other. In fashion this is achieved through textile selection and placement in a garment or range. A soft silk top may be the perfect feminine contrast to a pair of masculine tweed trousers. Balance is arranging elements so no one part of a design awkwardly overpowers the others. Balance may be symmetrical, asymmetrical or radial. The draped folds on an asymmetrical one-sleeve evening gown may radiate from the shoulder. Proportion evaluates the size and quantity of elements in a composition. The human body has its own proportions. A designer can use construction methods to emphasize or mask certain aspects of the human form through garment proportions. Unity is the overall effect achieved by all elements used in a garment, range or collection. Generally a designer will strive to create a harmonious and pleasing (therefore saleable) fashion collection. However some designers strive to use the elements and principles of design to create shocking, statement-making or disturbing collections. When creating a runway collection many fashion houses design one or two runway looks that sum up the design statement or unity of a collection, but are too outrageous or expensive to ever go into production.

DESIGNER SPOTLIGHT
RODARTE

Rodarte is a designer ready-to-wear line created by sisters Kate and Laura Mulleavy. The line is known for its fantastical surface treatments and construction methods. Surface treatments include hand-dyed gowns, stud encrusted accessories, and pictorial leather appliqués. Unusual construction methods include hand-knit decaying sweaters made from chain and leather. They are the only females, and the only Americans, to receive the prestigious Swiss Textile Award.

DISCUSSION QUESTIONS

1

The Mulleavy sisters went from being unknown to being on the cover of *WWD* basically overnight. How integral do you think their textile design was in their meteoric rise to success?

2

Though always highly acclaimed for their collections, some critics have noted 'that the designers focus on fabric at the expense of volume and silhouette' (<www.interviewmagazine.com>, 2010). Do you find this to be true?

3

Kate and Laura are hands-on in the creation of special couture textile effects for each collection. Do you think their work translated successfully in their mass-market collaborations with Target and Gap?

Shirred chartreuse leather.
Rodarte S/S 2013.

CHAPTER FIVE

Sourcing your Fabric

One of the most important aspects of delivering an amazing fashion product to your customer is the sourcing of your base materials. Once a designer has an idea of what textiles they want to create their collection with, they must know how to find the proper textile and where to purchase it from. There are many sources for fashion textiles. Finding the proper vendors will depend on the size of your company, the market level of your product and the type of textile you are looking for. A designer may find their sources changing with each seasonal collection or they may form a lasting relationship with a textile vendor. Most likely there will be a combination of both new and trusted sources as the business grows.

When designing for an already established brand a designer may be given a list of reliable vendors, specific textile properties and characteristics to look for and be less financially restricted in textile selection. An emerging designer will need to budget and source carefully, spending a considerable amount of time locating fabrics. Either way there will be a costing budget to refer to, to make sure the selected fabric does not exceed the projected manufacturing cost as this will affect both wholesale and eventual retail price. If a fabulous but expensive textile is found, a designer can simplify construction details to minimize cost or reduce the budget on a second textile as a truly fantastic fabric can carry a collection.

Quality is remembered long after the price is forgotten.
Gucci slogan

SOURCING AND SELECTING
TEXTILES FOR FASHION

CHAPTER ONE: THE ROLE OF TEXTILES IN FASHION
CHAPTER TWO: MATERIALS
CHAPTER THREE: SURFACE DESIGN
CHAPTER FOUR: CONCEPTUALIZING THE COLLECTION
CHAPTER FIVE: SOURCING YOUR FABRIC
CHAPTER SIX: TEXTILES AND THE COLLECTION
SOURCING INTERVIEWS
APPENDIX

134

TEXTILE SOURCES

All designers should set aside enough time each season to research the textile market, looking for the best fabrics to fit inspiration, trend and budget. It is especially important for a designer just starting out to explore all avenues of supply, collecting samples, cards and price lists. As a signature take on textiles begins to form after a few seasons, a design brand should have files of all sources both tried and untried that speak to their design aesthetic. These files will save time and energy in seasons to come. Not all vendors will work for all designers.

Primary sources

The primary sources for fashion textiles are mills, converters and importers. **Mills** own textile machinery and manufacture fabrics. They commonly specialize in either woven textiles or knit textiles, not both. There are mills that manufacture speciality fabrics or trims. Manufacturers that refine leather, suede or fur are called tanneries or furriers respectively. **Vertically integrated** mills source fibres, manufacture yarns, construct the fabrics and finish them.

Unfinished textiles are sold mainly to **converters**. Converters buy up large amounts of raw textiles called greige goods and have the fabrics dyed, printed or otherwise finished. A converter will often inform the mills on the type of construction methods to use while manufacturing the textile. Converters are not as common as they once were because many large mills have become vertically integrated.

Importers are mills and converters located in a foreign country. They operate in the same way as any in-country mill or converter. However, extra time and care must be taken when working with a non-local source. Always request sample yardage before ordering, research tariffs and trade laws for the exporting country and leave room in the production schedule in case the textile gets held in customs. Be aware that not all countries have textile standards laws; in these cases a sample of a few yards will not be sufficient to ensure the overall quality of the roll. When sourcing from such a country work with an importer you trust or an overseas agent (see p. 137). Textiles manufactured in other countries can also be sourced from a **direct importer** or vendor in your country of origin who imports and wholesales textiles from a variety of foreign sources. A direct importer is more like a jobber (see p. 136 for secondary sources) than a primary source and is a good way for a new designer to work with imported goods.

135

TEXTILE SOURCES
TEXTILE SHOWS AND INTERNET SOURCING
TEXTILE PROPERTIES
CUSTOM TEXTILE CREATION
STRATEGY
DESIGNER SPOTLIGHT – PROENZA SCHOULER

1 As cheaper production moves to Asia many US and European mills have closed down. Yolo Wool Mill in Woodland California is the last in its area.

Primary sources for fashion textiles are generally best for a well-established fashion brand. This category of vendor usually requires a high minimum yardage order that a small designer just will not be able to meet. These sources sell their textiles by the roll. Standard woven rolled textiles are generally 1.22 or 1.52 m (48 or 60 in) wide with 54.86 to 91.44 m (60 to 100 yd) lengths wrapped around an inner cardboard tube. Advances in manufacturing machines are now creating up to 2.54 m (100 in) widths and rolls of nearly 914.4 m (1,000 yd). Cut-and-sew knit fabrics are commonly sold open width or tubular in 16 to 23 kg (35 to 50 lb) rolls. It is not often that a primary source will sell small yardage amounts of a fabric unless it is **over run** inventory or **spot (nearby) goods** (fabrics nearly ready for sale but still being produced). Sometimes a smaller minimum can be negotiated at a higher price per yard. In order to survive some small mills and converters have made a practice of helping emerging designers by offering lower initial minimums in hopes of an ongoing relationship.

Primary sources not only sell the textile but also manufacture it. Because of this they often expect fabric to be pre-ordered by binding contract months ahead of time. By making textiles to order these companies cut down on costly prediction mistakes and fabric overages. For a designer, this kind of definite decision making well ahead of design season takes excellent target customer knowledge and confident colour and trend prediction. A well thought-out budget and secure financial resources will also be necessary. It is also helpful on the back end to have relationships with secondary sources that will purchase any remaining stock fabric.

**SOURCING AND SELECTING
TEXTILES FOR FASHION**

CHAPTER ONE: THE ROLE OF TEXTILES IN FASHION
CHAPTER TWO: MATERIALS
CHAPTER THREE: SURFACE DESIGN
CHAPTER FOUR: CONCEPTUALIZING THE COLLECTION
CHAPTER FIVE: SOURCING YOUR FABRIC
CHAPTER SIX: TEXTILES AND THE COLLECTION
SOURCING INTERVIEWS
APPENDIX

136

ENVIRONMENTAL CERTIFICATIONS

If environmental and humanitarian concerns are part of your branding concept don't forget to request documented proof of any certifications. It is important to ask what kinds of fibres are used and how they were produced. You will also want to know what the manufacturer's waste processes are and how their workers are treated. For more information on this refer back to Chapter 1.

Secondary sources

There are four secondary sources for textiles: jobbers, retail stores, brokers and the Internet. This section will address the first three; we will take a more in-depth look at Internet sourcing in the following section. Jobbers are the most likely source of textiles for a small design firm. Jobbers buy fabrics from mills, converters, importers and designers. A jobber will always have a rotating selection of textiles. Since they are not bound by the manufacturing process a jobber can carry many types of textiles at once, though many jobbers focus on textiles for one market segment. Some jobbers work exclusively with current textiles, buying a quantity of fabrics they think will be in demand and selling it in smaller amounts to several clients. It is always a good idea to ask who else has bought an obvious fabric as it would not be good to have the same exact print or textured textile as a direct competitor or nearby designer. Once you have established an ongoing relationship with a jobber it may be possible to ask them not to sell a specific fabric to anyone else that season, even if you won't be able to take it all. This is possible because there are other jobbers who work exclusively with over runs, discontinued mill or converter styles and designer seconds. You need to be careful when working with a jobber as there will be a finite amount of your selected textile. This is especially true when working with the seconds jobber; always make sure there is enough of a fabric to cover your projected sales estimates. Be careful to know if a fabric is a designer second. One, it won't do to put out a line created with a textile from a well-known designer's previous collection; two, if the fabric design is copyrighted there can be issues with using it in a professional capacity.

Retail stores are often the source for a home or hobby designer. A retail store will carry many fabrics but limited stock in each. Many retail stores buy their fabrics in 30 yard lengths or less. When fabrics are sold in these amounts they are folded in half lengthwise and rolled around a wide, flat piece of cardboard. Over-the-counter textile retailers in some large cities, like in New York's Garment District, are brick and mortar jobbers with a large selection of textiles on rolls. If you are in or nearby a large city it is well worth a trip to source from this type of retailer. Shorts, textile lengths of 40 yards or less, or remnants, 10 yards or less, can often be sourced from a jobber or over-the-counter retailer at a really good price. These lengths may be looked at when sourcing an accent or limited trim fabric for a collection or may make sense for a custom or accessories designer.

137

TEXTILE SOURCES
TEXTILE SHOWS AND INTERNET SOURCING
TEXTILE PROPERTIES
CUSTOM TEXTILE CREATION
STRATEGY
DESIGNER SPOTLIGHT – PROENZA SCHOULER

2 End-of-roll sourcing from a discount outlet is often a good way to cut costs for a young designer.

A broker is a middle man in the textile industry. They do not buy or house fabrics themselves but rather put a designer in touch with the appropriate textile source. They should be able to negotiate with vendors on behalf of a designer as they will have long-standing relationships with many sources in the industry. An overseas agent is a broker who resides in, or travels frequently to, a foreign country. It is advisable to work with an agent if you have never sourced overseas before, are unable to travel to the country yourself or have a tight budget that does not allow for the costly 'buyer beware' mistakes that can happen when sourcing non-locally. An overseas agent will know the import/export laws, have relationships with many mills and converters, can advise on local customs and be able to translate business agreements.

SOURCING AND SELECTING
TEXTILES FOR FASHION

CHAPTER ONE: THE ROLE OF TEXTILES IN FASHION
CHAPTER TWO: MATERIALS
CHAPTER THREE: SURFACE DESIGN
CHAPTER FOUR: CONCEPTUALIZING THE COLLECTION
CHAPTER FIVE: SOURCING YOUR FABRIC
CHAPTER SIX: TEXTILES AND THE COLLECTION
SOURCING INTERVIEWS
APPENDIX

138

ATTENDING A TRADE SHOW

What to bring: Tote bag for items collected, swatches of any previously selected textiles, photograph or print out of inspiration board, well-designed professional business card, binder with plastic sleeves for swatch sample organization, notebook, pens, small stapler, ID card, camera (always ask before using!).

What to do: Arrive early, sign up for seminars, review vendors online and try to set up appointments, buy a show catalogue, record textile categories, vendor sources and minimums, collect line and price sheets, staple vendors' business cards to swatches, note trends, and be courteous, professional and organized.

TEXTILE SHOWS AND INTERNET SOURCING

There are two easy ways to locate and contact myriad primary and secondary vendors. The traditional way is at textile trade shows, a more recent development is sourcing online through the Internet. Both offer a fast way to find the exact textile you are looking for. There are benefits to both that will be reviewed in this section.

Manufacturers can now easily be found that produce and finish textiles as well as construct the garment. Many of these vertically integrated manufacturers are located overseas. Working with overseas vendors can be a challenging experience but also has its advantages. Both trade shows and the Internet can be a great way for designers of all levels to find an overseas manufacturer to work with.

Trade shows

A trade show is a convention where vendors rent booths and display their product. In the fashion industry there are textile, manufacturing and wholesale trade shows. In this section we will be focusing on the first two. Textile and manufacturing vendors are often now found at the same shows due to the increase in vertically integrated manufacturing.

The most influential trade show is Première Vision (PV). This show traditionally takes place in Paris in February or March and September. However, New York, Japan, Shanghai, Beijing, Moscow and Sao Paulo all now offer some PV event (The Organizers: Première Vision, no date). Première Vision Pluriel in Paris is six shows: Première Vision (fabrics), Expofil (yarns and fibres), Indigo (textile design), ModAmont (textile accessories), Le Cuir à Paris (leather), Zoom by Fatex (fashion production). New York hosts Première Vision Preview previewing both PV and Indigo in January and July each year. The most recent addition is Denim by Première Vision, fully focused on the denim fabric and jeanswear market, showing in Paris in June and December. While these are the most well known of shows, more and more small, market-specific shows are springing up globally. Some of these may have expensive attendance fees or be invitation only; always check show information before travelling.

In addition to sourcing textile vendors, trade shows are excellent places to learn about textile developments, industry trends and gain design inspiration. Trade shows offer a schedule of seminars by fashion and trend gurus geared towards helping designers make textile selections. These are often free to show attendees but you may need to sign up ahead of time. In addition to the seminars there will usually be large trend displays in a centralized location.

139

TEXTILE SOURCES
TEXTILE SHOWS AND INTERNET SOURCING
TEXTILE PROPERTIES
CUSTOM TEXTILE CREATION
STRATEGY
DESIGNER SPOTLIGHT – PROENZA SCHOULER

A new designer should get to a trade show early, walk the entire show and note booths of interest. This will allow them to see what vendors are there, absorb trend information and lay out a plan for this season's sourcing. As a student or emerging designer you will not be able to access some of the more major exhibitors' stalls. Many will be closed to the general attendees as they only work with well-known designers or firms that can place large orders. Due to the increased ease with which textiles and prints are now knocked-off some exhibitors will be reluctant to show their product without an order. Though you may not be able to access everything, nothing beats the face to face connections you will make with vendors or the ability to touch and examine their wares.

Internet sourcing

The Internet has opened up non-local and overseas manufacturing and textile sourcing to designers of all levels. As a resource it is mainly free, all you need is an Internet connection and time. Unlike trade shows there are no entrance fees, travel expenses or time off work required. Sourcing on the Internet can happen twenty-four hours, seven days a week from any location on the globe.

A good place to start is using one of the high powered search engines, such as Google or Bing. Type in the specifics of the textile you are looking for plus the words 'fabric', 'textile', 'wholesaler', or 'manufacturer'. Scroll through both the web links, images and shopping. Though time consuming you can find the perfect textile without leaving your studio and often comparatively price shop. Websites for textile or fashion clubs and schools can often offer good links to vendors. Professional directories such as Alibaba.com and GlobalSources.com can lead to mills and converters. Blogs on textiles and fashion can often turn up good information. Local sources can be found by entering your location and the words 'jobber', 'mill' or 'converter'.

For an emerging designer the Internet can save a lot of man-hours. Craft a well thought-out contact letter asking about samples and swatches, textile minimums, delivery turnaround and shipping costs. This standard letter can be copied and pasted over and over when reaching out to vendors. Be sure to tailor it to the specifics of the company you are contacting. Upon receiving a positive response, ask for their current swatch book and price list to add to your files. Often you may be able to reach smaller vendors who are willing to accept modest minimum orders as they cannot afford travel expenses for major shows. While these connections may be mutually beneficial take care to have a back-up plan in case it does not work out. It is very easy to promise delivery and quality assurances over the Internet to a faceless consumer.

1 Booth display at Denim by Première Vision trade show in Paris.

2 The Internet has opened up international textile sourcing to designers of all levels. Some websites like eco-focused Source4Style.com help designers navigate this resource.

**SOURCING AND SELECTING
TEXTILES FOR FASHION**

CHAPTER ONE: THE ROLE OF TEXTILES IN FASHION
CHAPTER TWO: MATERIALS
CHAPTER THREE: SURFACE DESIGN
CHAPTER FOUR: CONCEPTUALIZING THE COLLECTION
CHAPTER FIVE: SOURCING YOUR FABRIC
CHAPTER SIX: TEXTILES AND THE COLLECTION
SOURCING INTERVIEWS
APPENDIX

140

TEXTILE PROPERTIES

Textile properties affect how the fabric interacts with the human form and ultimately the consumer. Properties fall into two categories: functional and aesthetic. In order to source the proper textile a designer must be able to speak intelligently about the type of fabric they are looking for. This requires a learned language of fabric properties. By being able to relay clearly their vision in industry terminology a designer will have an easier time sourcing remotely through a jobber, broker or the Internet. This terminology will also help project a professional appearance when sourcing face to face at an over-the-counter retailer or a trade show.

Functional properties

The functional properties of a textile are characteristics that affect fabric performance and special construction considerations. Fibre content and textile construction methods will always impact the performance of the final textile. When selecting a textile ensure each component equals the end result you are looking for. For example, natural fibres have more breathability but less wrinkle resistance than synthetic fibres, woven fabrics will hold shape and tailoring while knits drape naturally.

Durability of a textile is important. While very few fashion garments are expected to be worn until they wear out, the consumer will expect a good amount of time to pass with the garment in 'like new' condition. When speaking of durability a designer should be concerned with abrasion resistance, pilling, colour fastness and fabric retention. Drape is how a fabric falls in space. A thinner gauge yarn loosely woven or knit will fall softly and gracefully, a thicker yarn in a tighter construction will crease, fold and retain some structure when draped. The structure of a fabric can be inherent in the textile fibre and construction or manipulated during garment design. Structure is the ability of a fabric to resist gravity; it is the opposite of drape. Seams, darts, interfacing and supports can improve a textile's structural property during garment construction. A fabric's cover or opacity is an important factor in determining both garment finishing methods and possible collection additions. The best way to determine a fabric's cover is to lay it over a textile of opposite value. A non-opaque black fabric laid over a white will show the weave and opacity level of the cover textile. When using a sheer fabric in a collection interior seaming methods must be clean finished. If a blouse is constructed from a sheer material an opaque shell may be added to the line for a more modest consumer. Drape, structure and cover are all secondary functions of a textile's weight or thickness.

Finally, special performance properties can be added to a textile during synthetic fibre engineering or the finishing process. Common engineered properties include wrinkle, water and fire resistance, UV protection, and temperature regulation.

1 (opposite) Both the leather used for the bodice and tulle used for the skirt offer structure in their own way. Primrose Rayneese.

141

TEXTILE SOURCES
TEXTILE SHOWS AND INTERNET SOURCING
TEXTILE PROPERTIES
CUSTOM TEXTILE CREATION
STRATEGY
DESIGNER SPOTLIGHT – PROENZA SCHOULER

1

**SOURCING AND SELECTING
TEXTILES FOR FASHION**

CHAPTER ONE: THE ROLE OF TEXTILES IN FASHION
CHAPTER TWO: MATERIALS
CHAPTER THREE: SURFACE DESIGN
CHAPTER FOUR: CONCEPTUALIZING THE COLLECTION
CHAPTER FIVE: SOURCING YOUR FABRIC
CHAPTER SIX: TEXTILES AND THE COLLECTION
SOURCING INTERVIEWS
APPENDIX

142

Aesthetic properties

The aesthetic properties of a fabric are the characteristics that affect the appearance of a textile. Some aesthetic properties, such as a printed pattern lining up at the seams, will need to be considered when constructing a garment. The manufacturing process of a fibre to yarn will ultimately inform the texture of a final fashion textile. Combed/worsted yarns have been processed in a way to create a uniformly finished, smooth yarn and textile. Carded and woollen yarns will be coarser and have a bit of fuzzy nap. Depending on the knit or woven method of construction these factors will be enhanced or restrained. While a combed yarn may seem the default property for sophisticated fashion, depending on style trends a designer may seek a carded yarn textile, which will give a more rustic look.

2 Matching the seams in the construction of a garment, using a fabric such as this, is just one aesthetic consideration!

143

TEXTILE SOURCES
TEXTILE SHOWS AND INTERNET SOURCING
TEXTILE PROPERTIES
CUSTOM TEXTILE CREATION
STRATEGY
DESIGNER SPOTLIGHT – PROENZA SCHOULER

As previously discussed, colour is perhaps the number one issue affecting garment selection. When discussing colour with a textile dealer there are three characteristics to be aware of: trend (does the dealer have the seasonal palette?); colour fastness (are the dyes and printing mediums resistant to wash and light fading?); and permeability (does the dye or print look the same on both sides of the fabric?). If you are designing a high wear-and-wash item such as a shirt or casual pants, thorough dye and print penetration will help avoid worn and faded areas. The texture of a fashion textile is a direct result of yarn selection and construction methods. These things should be taken into consideration during the design conception because they affect both aesthetics and function of a textile. Texture is not just a visual aesthetic but also a tactile one influencing the hand or feel of a fabric. A fabric with a lot of texture will most likely be a warmer fabric; it may not feel as nice directly on the skin and may require a lining. Often an interesting texture will be paired with a simpler design as it may be too busy to add additional design details. Print and pattern are aesthetic properties that can add artistry and drama to a collection. A spot-on patterned textile can help sell a collection but a poor choice can ruin an otherwise fantastic design.

SOURCING AND SELECTING
TEXTILES FOR FASHION

CHAPTER ONE: THE ROLE OF TEXTILES IN FASHION
CHAPTER TWO: MATERIALS
CHAPTER THREE: SURFACE DESIGN
CHAPTER FOUR: CONCEPTUALIZING THE COLLECTION
CHAPTER FIVE: SOURCING YOUR FABRIC
CHAPTER SIX: TEXTILES AND THE COLLECTION
SOURCING INTERVIEWS
APPENDIX

144

> The only new work you can do in fashion is via technology. It lets you create something you couldn't have done in the past.
> Hussein Chalayan

CUSTOM TEXTILE CREATION

Custom textile creation is an important part of designing a collection. Whether a designer does it themselves, hires someone else to design to their vision or purchases the rights to a particular fabric, few things set a collection apart from the pack like innovative and original textiles. A designer must start early with sourcing when adding a custom textile into a seasonal collection. Unless the customized fabric is being supplied by a mill or converter, not only will the base textile need to be sourced but also the surface design house. If you plan on customizing the fabric on your own this may require even more time for experimentation and production.

Customization and the computer

Within the fashion industry the computer has become as important a design tool as traditional art, design and sewing supplies. Not only can a designer use the computer through the Internet to source vendors but they can also access a much broader world of inspiration and information. Websites like Style.com and Catwalking.com shoot and post all the important designer fashion shows allowing an emerging designer unlimited access to what is happening in the top tier of the industry. Trend sites can help a designer narrow down what they are seeing. Once a design team has an idea about the type of textures, colours and surface designs, moving forward they can use the computer to resource how and where to customize their textiles. If a designer is planning on customizing a fabric themselves many online instructional PDFs, blog postings and tutorial videos can be found, which enable a designer to become essentially self taught.

In addition to helping conceptualize a custom textile through online resources, the computer is a powerful offline tool. Many computer programs have been created that allow a designer to build a textile in virtual space and send the plans to a production house or manufacturer to realize the physical product. There are many high powered and expensive programs on the market that can produce very specific instructions. However, by using some creativity, a designer can use a combination of reference photographs, written instructions and basic graphics software to produce original textile designs, repeat patterns, dye-flow ideas and colour combinations. They can then use the computer to send these tech packages to the proper vendor and get their customized textile into production.

1

1 Creating a new textile through texture: Nomadic Wonderland, deconstructed dress. Wool felt, recycled wool felt. Laser cutting and mixture of handcraft skills, Eunsuk Hur 2009.

2

2 'The Color-In Dress' digital print. Design and concept: Berber Soepboer; textile design/graphic design: Michiel Schuurman.

**SOURCING AND SELECTING
TEXTILES FOR FASHION**

CHAPTER ONE: THE ROLE OF TEXTILES IN FASHION
CHAPTER TWO: MATERIALS
CHAPTER THREE: SURFACE DESIGN
CHAPTER FOUR: CONCEPTUALIZING THE COLLECTION
CHAPTER FIVE: SOURCING YOUR FABRIC
CHAPTER SIX: TEXTILES AND THE COLLECTION
SOURCING INTERVIEWS
APPENDIX

146

Traditional methods of customization

There are numerous ways to add a custom textile to a collection. One of the most common is to purchase a textile and add surface design elements. For a broader look at surface design methods please refer back to Chapter 3. If a designer or design team is too busy designing the collection to also design the textiles, there are still ways to get a great customized textile on your line. Depending on your size, notoriety and financial backing a mill or converter may be willing to sell you a textile from their current line and make it unavailable to anyone else for that season or within your market segmentation. For example, your design team may be the only ones creating contemporary cocktail dresses with a custom textile but the mill can still sell it to a lingerie manufacturer.

A designer can also walk the print and pattern trade shows such as Printsource or Première Vision's Indigo. There you will be able to purchase a custom print from a textile design house or small designer. There will also be vendors who trade in non-copyrighted vintage clothing and textiles. A designer can purchase a fantastic pillow case from the 1930s and have an embroidery house knock off the detailing for a collection of sundresses. An alternative way to utilize vintage textiles in a fashion collection is to upcycle. Upcycling is an offshoot of sustainability in fashion in which a designer will create new textiles or garments from an already manufactured and used or worn textile.

Collaborations can be another way to inexpensively create a terrific design just for your collection. We have already looked at collaborations of well-known designers with mass-market retailers, such as, Missoni/Target. Customization collaborations work much in the same way. A design brand would reach out to another artist and offer an upfront payment, a percentage of sales or a certain amount of end product to create custom weaves, knits, patterns or graphics. At times reasonable press barter may be made depending on the popularity of the design brand and whether the collaboration will raise the profile of the artist.

The customization of a textile and how often that textile is used by a designer can lead to a textile **signature** for a design brand. A signature textile can be one continuous use of the same exact graphic or pattern. Think of the Louis Vuitton initial and floral repeat or Burberry's plaid. Chanel too is known for its woven textiles in a colour range based mainly on black and white (see page 151).

147

TEXTILE SOURCES
TEXTILE SHOWS AND INTERNET SOURCING
TEXTILE PROPERTIES
CUSTOM TEXTILE CREATION
STRATEGY
DESIGNER SPOTLIGHT – PROENZA SCHOULER

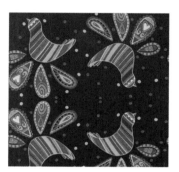

3 To design a custom textile pattern the designer a) researches inspiration; b) creates an image; and c) takes that image into repeat and offer it in other colour ways. Courtesy of Caroline Kaufman.

4 Sustainable fashion line, Soham Dave, works with local Indian artisans to create custom fabrics through traditional block print, dye and embroidery techniques.

5 Upcycled dress from vintage men's ties. Pratt Institute, undergraduate work by Hannah Ross.

SOURCING AND SELECTING
TEXTILES FOR FASHION

CHAPTER ONE: THE ROLE OF TEXTILES IN FASHION
CHAPTER TWO: MATERIALS
CHAPTER THREE: SURFACE DESIGN
CHAPTER FOUR: CONCEPTUALIZING THE COLLECTION
CHAPTER FIVE: SOURCING YOUR FABRIC
CHAPTER SIX: TEXTILES AND THE COLLECTION
SOURCING INTERVIEWS
APPENDIX

148

Luck is what happens when preparation meets opportunity.

Lucius Annaeus Seneca,
Roman philosopher

STRATEGY

Purchasing textiles for producing a collection is one of the largest costs associated with the fashion business. Through detailed planning a designer will realize what their textile budget is and source accordingly. There are some ways to cut costs, but an emerging designer wishing to debut their first collection needs to be aware of the sometimes prohibitive costs associated with producing even a limited line of garments. Fabulous designs, stunning textiles and putting on an attention grabbing show are only part of the equation to running a successful fashion business. Understanding cash flow, when in the design cycle it will be needed and where to get it, are essential to keeping a fashion business alive. The more prepared a designer is prior to starting the business of fashion, the more time they have in season to focus on the creation of fashion.

The business plan

All businesses benefit from looking ahead at projected specifics of brand, target market, manufacturing and budget. The result of researching, assembling and recording these projections is called a **business plan**. A good business plan can help refine and solidify a fashion brand's design theory. When approached one section at a time, planning and writing a business plan will often go quicker than expected. There are many books, websites and articles on the subject of business planning. The Small Business Administration in the US and Federation of Small Businesses in the UK are free resources where a designer can attend seminars or talk with a seasoned industry professional.

All business plans follow the same basic outline, fleshed out with the specifics of the individual brand. When reading a business plan the first section will be the **Executive Summary**. The executive summary will introduce the reader to the brand and summarize the highlights of what the plan covers. As a result it is best to write the executive summary last, once all research has been completed and assembled. After the executive summary comes **The Brand**. The brand section should include details about your company including the mission statement, the design vision, product segmentation, market segmentation and market level. This section should also state what type of legal business structure it is, for example a corporation or partnership, the business or fashion experience of the principles involved and start-up plans.

149

TEXTILE SOURCES
TEXTILE SHOWS AND INTERNET SOURCING
TEXTILE PROPERTIES
CUSTOM TEXTILE CREATION
STRATEGY
DESIGNER SPOTLIGHT – PROENZA SCHOULER

Next will be **Target Market** and **Market Analysis**. These sections may be combined or written separately. They will cover an in-depth look at who the brand is designing for, including information such as sex, age, income/education, location and interests. There should be a closer look at market segmentation and intended clothing style. Lastly, pulling facts from government and business websites, the plan will analyse what is the economic climate of the appointed market, who are the brand's direct competitors and what the brand has to offer that is unique. Finally there should be a **Marketing Plan** covering how the brand will reach its intended market. It should describe the number of seasonal collections, runway shows or market appointments, contacting and attracting press (publications, blogs), tags, logos, advertising, pricing and point of sale (web, brick and mortar, wholesale or retail).

The second half of the business plan gets into the particulars of running the business. It starts with **Operations**, detailing the day-to-day operating procedures. This should be as detailed as possible, projecting forward all aspects needed to produce your fashion line. Included should be studio location, hours of operation, equipment (what you have and what is needed), materials, production processes, staffing positions, inventory control and sales. Operations will contain a costing outlook for each operation. Be as accurate as possible and always round up. Next is **Implementation and Management**, the how and who of operating your business. Outline the calendar year in terms of projects and when they need to be completed, list functions to perform, equipment needed, budget available and which staff member(s) will handle each part. **Financials**, the final section of a business plan, is the most important. Many start ups and entrepreneurs are overwhelmed when faced with the forward thinking and maths involved in this section. It is advisable to reach out to a certified accountant or business mentor to review the financial projections. Many small businesses go under while turning a profit because they do not understand cash flow strategies. **Cash flow** equations should cover an entire operating year. The first month will have to include start-up costs needed to get operational. All months should include starting cash, amount of garments per line, price of each item, monthly sales, manufacturing and overhead costs, profit from sales, sales growth, percentage of sales on credit, collection schedule, and inventory balance. A plan should then project a three-to-five year **profit and loss schedule**, minusing all expenses from projected sales profit times yearly sales growth. Often a company will not see a profit until year two; if by year three profits are nominal you may want to reconsider the viability of your business model.

**SOURCING AND SELECTING
TEXTILES FOR FASHION**

CHAPTER ONE: THE ROLE OF TEXTILES IN FASHION
CHAPTER TWO: MATERIALS
CHAPTER THREE: SURFACE DESIGN
CHAPTER FOUR: CONCEPTUALIZING THE COLLECTION
CHAPTER FIVE: SOURCING YOUR FABRIC
CHAPTER SIX: TEXTILES AND THE COLLECTION
SOURCING INTERVIEWS
APPENDIX

150

Funding sources

Upon completing the business plan and financial outlook of the company, many emerging designers will realize they do not have the personal resources needed to make it through the first year. At this point it will be time to consider funding options. These options fall into two groups, **partnerships** and **loans**. A third group could be considered, **free money**. This would be personal gifts, grants and awards. However nothing is ever free; these monies may cost in strings attached, stringent procedural requirements and/or preparation time spent vs. probability of award.

Financial partnership occurs when a creative principal partners with a business principal. This can be an advantageous situation for an emerging designer on many levels, both financial and operational. Be sure to research prior business background and personal credit of anyone you go into business with. Be aware that many people have an interest in fashion but not the creative eye, so lay out in detail the amount of creative and business control each partner will have. **Angel investors** are a somewhat new form of partnership where someone with an interest in fashion and money to invest may be looking to fund a creative business. This may be purely philanthropic or the investor may have other motivations; make sure to get all agreements in writing and looked over by a lawyer.

Loans are the traditional way many small businesses get start-up cash. A good place to begin looking for money is a **family and friends** loan – these will be either partial or full amount of monies needed, funded by personal contacts who know the designer. The advantage of this may be a more flexible payment schedule and no or little interest. A **small business loan** would be granted by a bank with a set payment and interest amortization schedule. Bank loans are hard to come by these days for a start-up company with no financial history. Some start-up costs can be offset using the personal credit of the principals involved in the business. The two ways to do this would be through vendor **Net 30** where a business will not have to pay for materials upfront but will be given a credited grace period of time, generally 30 days but up to 120. The other way would be **credit cards**. This can be a slippery slope and it is advisable to be honest with yourself about the way you handle money owed and bill payments. Lastly, once operational to the point of showing your sample line, a business can often get a **loan on POS**. This is where a company would go to a lender with their seasonal purchase orders and borrow the money needed to manufacture based on order amounts placed. One of the places to go is a **factor**. A factor is a traditional financial middle man in business who, based on issues like receivables, purchase orders and business history, provides cash flow for a fee.

151

TEXTILE SOURCES
TEXTILE SHOWS AND INTERNET SOURCING
TEXTILE PROPERTIES
CUSTOM TEXTILE CREATION
STRATEGY
DESIGNER SPOTLIGHT – PROENZA SCHOULER

1 Chanel, the classic fashion house, forged many business partnerships, such as with businessman Pierre Wertheimer in 1924 and with jeweller Robert Goossens in 1953.

**SOURCING AND SELECTING
TEXTILES FOR FASHION**

**DESIGNER
SPOTLIGHT**
PROENZA SCHOULER

152

Proenza Schouler is a womenswear and accessories brand by design duo Jack McCollough and Lazaro Hernandez. The brand launched in 2002 and quickly became known for its youth inspired surface treatments and custom textile developments. Proenza Schouler takes chances with its print, texture and textile mixtures every season but its classic tailoring and silhouettes ground each collection.

DISCUSSION QUESTIONS

1

Proenza Schouler employs Alejandro Cardenas, a fine artist, as its art director and textile designer. How important a role do you think fine art skills (drawing, painting, sculpture) play in a successful fashion line?

2

In 2008, interior textile house Knoll Inc. had Jack and Lazaro design a line of interior fabrics for their Knoll Luxe division. The line was based on textiles straight from the Proenza Schouler runway collections. Do you have enough interest in textiles to find this type of opportunity appealing? Why or why not?

3

Lazaro stated in a 9 January 2013 interview with *WWD*, 'A lot of the shapes that can be worn have already been created. It's not about three sleeves or three pant legs or anything like that. For us, it's about the surface. That's what the future of fashion is. It's technology.' What do you think about his opinion? (Iredale, 2013).

A selection of looks from Proenza
Schouler S/S 2012 RTW collection.

CHAPTER SIX

Textiles and the Collection

Moving forward with full knowledge of the critical role of textile in fashion, a designer begins to build their new collection. The act of design starts in the subconscious; often when asked to clarify how they create what they do, the artist will first come to the conclusion that it is purely instinctual. Upon further examination comes the realization that information, education and experience have honed their abilities to take a good idea and make great fashion. The Greek philosopher Aristotle said, 'We are what we repeatedly do, excellence then is not an act, but a habit.' This holds true not only in life but also in design. The more critical thinking and practical experience a designer puts behind each collection, the stronger the resulting designs will be.

In this chapter we will take a look at how to put the information presented in this book into practice. We will touch on each of the major steps a designer takes when moving from inspiration to production. At each step the role of textile will be examined. In this way, theoretical information will become applied knowledge as you move forward in your own design career.

Design is the method of putting form and content together. Design, just as art, has multiple definitions; there is no single definition. Design can be art. Design can be aesthetics. Design is so simple, that's why it is so complicated.
Paul Rand

**SOURCING AND SELECTING
TEXTILES FOR FASHION**

CHAPTER ONE: THE ROLE OF TEXTILES IN FASHION
CHAPTER TWO: MATERIALS
CHAPTER THREE: SURFACE DESIGN
CHAPTER FOUR: CONCEPTUALIZING THE COLLECTION
CHAPTER FIVE: SOURCING YOUR FABRIC
CHAPTER SIX: TEXTILES AND THE COLLECTION
SOURCING INTERVIEWS
APPENDIX

156

Appropriateness reflects the degree of 'fit' that an object has with place, function, user, maker and environment. The result should be a selection of materials appropriate to their expected lifetime's task; the development of design strategies such as versatility and reparability to keep a product relevant; the promotion of emotional bonds with a product which encourage ongoing use; and an overall sensitivity to how fabrics and garments are actually used.
Kate Fletcher, Sustainable Fashion and Textiles

TEXTILE SELECTION AND GARMENT DESIGN

Each pre-season as a designer gets ready to design their next collection, textiles and trims will need to be selected. The selection of textiles will be based on specific criterion unique to each designer and each collection. Some of these standards will be variable season to season, while others will remain static forming the basis of the brand's design aesthetic. Once the catalogue of guidelines has been established, the designer will contact their sources, select their fabrics and begin the design process.

Static guidelines for textile selection

Every design house has a number of facts that influence its design theory. These ethoses form the basis of the brand identity, which will directly impact textile selection. Static guidelines are unchanging; they will remain no matter the inspiration, trend or season. At times a certain textile or print will have such influence on a designer that it will become part of the brand's identity working its way into each collection.

The static guidelines a designer must be aware of when sourcing textiles are market segmentation, target market, ethics and budget. Market segmentation refers to the overall category of design. Some of the categories to keep in mind will be: men's or women's, ready to wear or streetwear, couture or mass market. A men's streetwear brand may never have use for silk shantung but may need a trending denim in every collection. Target market is the exact customer the house is designing for. A designer will need to be aware of the specific textile properties that attract their consumer. Ethics are starting to play a significant role in many designer collections. Some things to be aware of when sourcing are locality, manufacturing processes, base materials, and who is creating the textile as well as care, longevity and recyclability of the final garment. Finally, the budget will play a major role in the selection of a textile. A designer's budget may increase as the years go by, however, the retail price of the garments should not fluctuate with business growth. It is necessary to create a costing formula for manufacturing and projected retail price from the beginning, which will remain static. This budget will remain static because market segmentation, target market and ethics of a brand should not change with company growth.

157

TEXTILE SELECTION AND GARMENT DESIGN
DRAWING YOUR DESIGNS
DRAPING AND PATTERNMAKING
PREPARING FOR PRODUCTION
EDITING THE COLLECTION
DESIGNER SPOTLIGHT – ISSEY MIYAKE

1 A designer will source a variety of seasonal textiles to invoke the feeling of their inspiration. Courtesy of Caroline Kaufman.

Variable guidelines for textile selection

Many factors that affect textile selection will change with each collection produced. Influences that change or fluctuate season to season are referred to as variable. The variable guidelines a designer should take into consideration when selecting their textiles are trend, availability, inspiration, season and garment design.

As explored in Chapter 4 fashion trends are ever changing and at the same time somewhat cyclical. How much or how little trend influences a collection will depend in part on the static ethos of a brand. However, since the manufacturing mills do follow strict trend research, the textiles, patterns and colours available on the market are trend oriented. Not only will trend affect the availability of textiles but so too will the vendor source and company size. Certain sources may only carry limited amounts of a chosen textile and a small designer may only be able to afford to source from these vendors. Inspiration will influence heavily a designer's textile selection. A designer should take into consideration fashion era, colour, texture, pattern and mood and fit textiles into the story. The season affects the weight and hand of selected textiles due to weather and temperature considerations. Seasonal weather influences may shift according to location of both the design brand and target market.

Garment design plans for the collection will play a major role in the selection of textiles. designer designs first and then sources textile or sources first and designs to textile selection, they must have some idea of intended design plans prior to sourcing. Silhouette, construction details and surface design will all play a part in what is an acceptable material to work with. While some textiles are universally adaptable, fabrics with obvious specialty properties will be only acceptable in some applications. For example, special fabrics with a high nap, extreme heavy or light weight, sheer opacity, special finish, and that are patterned or heavily textured will all require sheer construction considerations.

SOURCING AND SELECTING
TEXTILES FOR FASHION

CHAPTER ONE: THE ROLE OF TEXTILES IN FASHION
CHAPTER TWO: MATERIALS
CHAPTER THREE: SURFACE DESIGN
CHAPTER FOUR: CONCEPTUALIZING THE COLLECTION
CHAPTER FIVE: SOURCING YOUR FABRIC
CHAPTER SIX: TEXTILES AND THE COLLECTION
SOURCING INTERVIEWS
APPENDIX

158

DRAWING YOUR DESIGNS

Once a designer is clear on seasonal trend and inspiration and knows their brand objectives, they can begin planning the line. Though a fashion garment is a three-dimensional object the planning stages often take place in a two-dimensional space. Traditionally a collection would be planned through a series of hand-drawn fashion illustrations, these days many designers choose to use computerized tools. No matter the method, it is necessary for a designer to take the plans out of their head and finalize them on paper. This allows a clear look in the light of day at how their ideas may play out. The success of a line will depend on careful detailed planning, what seems like a great colour combination in the conceptual stages may look different when placed into an illustration. Fantastical design silhouettes may be reinforced as avant-garde genius when drawn out or realized as costume not fashion. Therefore learning to express design ideas through fashion illustration is a required skill.

The fashion figure

When illustrating a fashion idea it must be drawn on a human figure. It is typical in fashion illustration to elongate the proportions of the human body and exaggerate the gesture. A fashion figure will be 9–10 heads high, rather than the realistic 7.5 or 8 heads used in figure drawing. The breakdown of sections will be in thirds, split at waist and knee, rather than two, split at the symphysis. The head should always be 1 head high, in a 10-head figure the extra measurement is added to the bottom proportion. In male figures the torso should gain the extra head and muscle tone should be pronounced. Stance should always be balanced over a vertical centre line so the figure does not appear to lean unrealistically. Horizontal movement lines should be placed at shoulder, waist and knee, tilted in a realistic relationship to each other. Details like hair, facial features, hands and feet may be simplified but must be indicated. It is a good idea to develop a series of fashion body templates or croquis that can be traced and worked upon season after season to speed the design process. Individualized style can play a big part in the attractiveness of your illustrations, which can then become part of your brand's promotional package.

159

TEXTILE SELECTION AND GARMENT DESIGN
DRAWING YOUR DESIGNS
DRAPING AND PATTERNMAKING
PREPARING FOR PRODUCTION
EDITING THE COLLECTION
DESIGNER SPOTLIGHT – ISSEY MIYAKE

1 Hand-drawn fashion figures.
Courtesy of Semaj Bryant.

Hand illustration

Drawing a fashion illustration by hand will give the advantage of fluidity, line weight change and attitude over the exactness of computerized programs. These components make up the gesture of a drawing. Gesture should focus on simplified movement rather than detailed minuteness. In fashion illustration, the less line used to express your ideas the better, quickness and skill will be achieved over time with repetitive practice. Thought should be given to the overall mood of the drawing and what it has to say about the final garment design.

Mood and rapidity of drawing style are enhanced by fluid and expressive drawing mediums. Traditionally, soft pencil or oil pastels, pen and inks, watercolour or gouache were used while drawing from a live model. For many modern designers a selection of professional markers with varying tip sizes have replaced more traditional mediums. While it is still optimal to draw from life, fashion photography has offered a reasonable replacement to an in-studio model. Clear shots of runway models can be sourced from fashion magazines or websites. A variety of surface mediums may be used but bristol in a velum finish will be universally receptive to many drawing mediums. Its smooth surface will aid in the flow of a rapidly drawn fashion figure.

In fashion illustration care should be taken for proper expression of garment proportion and detailing, especially if the designer is working with a design team comprised of a separate patternmaker or technical designer. Notes may be added to the borders of a fashion sketch to clarify intentions. Finalized fashion illustrations of the type to be used in promotional materials should focus on the overall composition of the illustration. Where and how much of the figure is placed on the page; the play of positive and negative space (figure vs. environment); light and shadow; and detail focus will all help to convey the mood of the design.

A designer must also learn to convey fabric type and detail clearly. Colour should match textile as closely as possible. Different mediums may be considered for their usefulness in illustrating fabric types. For example, a medium that can be built up on the page like gouache may be preferable for a textured fabric rendering. Highlights and shadows should be commensurate with those found on the actual textile. When working with a patterned textile care should be taken both in proportional representation and likeness of actual print.

**SOURCING AND SELECTING
TEXTILES FOR FASHION**

CHAPTER ONE: THE ROLE OF TEXTILES IN FASHION
CHAPTER TWO: MATERIALS
CHAPTER THREE: SURFACE DESIGN
CHAPTER FOUR: CONCEPTUALIZING THE COLLECTION
CHAPTER FIVE: SOURCING YOUR FABRIC
CHAPTER SIX: TEXTILES AND THE COLLECTION
SOURCING INTERVIEWS
APPENDIX

160

Computer aided illustration

The acceptance of computerized illustrations in the fashion world has helped many a designer lacking in traditional hand skills. The computer is an amazing tool that once learned can subtract many hours from the process of drawing out a line. For those designers who simply cannot get the hang of drawing the human form, there is the option of scanning in a photograph, tracing the human form and then using some program tools to stretch the drawing into the correct fashion proportions. These croquis, once perfected, can be saved in files and used over and over again, each time being 'saved as' to create a new file without changing the original one.

A nice option to include some computerized work into a fashion illustration is through the use of a Wacom tablet, a flat sensitized drawing surface that once plugged into a computer records the gestures 'drawn' on it into a computerized file. This allows some of the beauty of a hand-drawn image to be incorporated into a design programme though the computer ultimately decides on line weight and small detail inclusion. A clean hand-drawn image can be scanned into the computer. It is advisable to trace line work clearly in ink, erasing all extraneous pencil markings and smudges or to retrace the figure onto clean paper prior to scanning for best results. A third option is to draw the figure in the computer using the mouse and an illustration or drawing program.

161

TEXTILE SELECTION AND GARMENT DESIGN
DRAWING YOUR DESIGNS
DRAPING AND PATTERNMAKING
PREPARING FOR PRODUCTION
EDITING THE COLLECTION
DESIGNER SPOTLIGHT – ISSEY MIYAKE

2

2 CAD programs allow scanned swatches of your actual textile to be added into your fashion illustration. Courtesy of Hana Pak.

COMPUTER AIDED DESIGN

Computer Aided Design programs function through one of two 'languages': vector or bitmap. Illustration programs run in vector where strokes and shapes are plotted on an x/y axis allowing for proportionate up or down scaling of a graphic's size without loss of detail. Photo realistic programs use raster, or bitmap, where images are plotted on a pixelated grid matrix that allows for realistic colour blending but images lose definition when resized.

Once the clothed figure is in the destination file with all details outlined, check to see that all line work forms closed shapes. This will allow for easy shape selection with program tools. You will then be able to fill closed areas with colours, patterns or scanned fabrics. When scanning repetitive textured, patterned or plain fabrics, scan at a high resolution, open in the program and find the repeat. Mark the repeat with guidelines, select, copy and paste into a new file. Reduce that file in size to make it proportional to the illustration, save as a pattern and use it to fill. For a non-repetitive textile, draw the guidelines smaller than the actual scan, select an organic shape covering the right edge and copy and paste it over the left edge. Repeat, selecting top and covering bottom edges. Then the selection edges will create a seamless repeat when tiled. Swatches containing incomplete pattern repeats may need to be built up using the paint tools in a program.

SOURCING AND SELECTING
TEXTILES FOR FASHION

CHAPTER ONE: THE ROLE OF TEXTILES IN FASHION
CHAPTER TWO: MATERIALS
CHAPTER THREE: SURFACE DESIGN
CHAPTER FOUR: CONCEPTUALIZING THE COLLECTION
CHAPTER FIVE: SOURCING YOUR FABRIC
CHAPTER SIX: TEXTILES AND THE COLLECTION
SOURCING INTERVIEWS
APPENDIX

162

DRAPING AND PATTERNMAKING

Once the plans have been laid for the direction of a collection, it is time to realize each individual design. This is done through draping, patternmaking and toile. Using the illustration as map, the designer or patternmaker will begin to plot the steps to take the two-dimensional textile and build a three-dimensional garment. Knowledge of textile properties and garment construction are imperative. At least a swatch of all textiles to be used in the collection should be present in the studio as the design process moves into this stage. Being able to see, touch and handle the textile will increase the understanding of what its capabilities are and how to utilize them in realizing the final garment.

Draping

Draping is the act of manipulating textile on a dress dummy or live model to create fashion designs. Some designers prefer this to the act of designing by illustrative method; some use it in conjunction with illustration to clarify textile capabilities; and some use it in place of flat patternmaking. When using draping to design a collection it is advisable to use a less expensive fabric than the one intended for the final garment. Muslin or inexpensive unbleached woven cotton is a great stand in. Muslin comes in various weights and YPI (yarns per inch) and can represent most fabrics. However, if there are distinct properties that will differ drastically from this type of fabric to final fabric, make sure to source an inexpensive but representational textile for the actual fabric. If a textile has an extreme drape or heavy weight, an equivalent substitute should be sourced.

When draping use a dress form whose proportions represent your ideal client. Dress forms can be custom made to a designer's specifications, though this can get expensive. It is best to try to find a company that makes a form close to your ideals. Order the one in the middle of your sizing scale. This way your draped designs can easily be graded up and down, covering all size categories without distortion.

In addition to a dress form and fabric, a designer will also want to have on hand a sharp pair of fabric scissors, plenty of straight pins, tailor's chalk and a handheld needle and thread. Work methodically and slowly, using the scissors and tailor's chalk to mark important aspects of the design and connection points in the fabric. Remember the textile will eventually need to be removed from the body and traced or recorded into a flat paper pattern for production. It is a good idea to take clear photographs of the design from all sides while still on the form. Move in for close-up detailed areas.

163

TEXTILE SELECTION AND GARMENT DESIGN
DRAWING YOUR DESIGNS
DRAPING AND PATTERNMAKING
PREPARING FOR PRODUCTION
EDITING THE COLLECTION
DESIGNER SPOTLIGHT – ISSEY MIYAKE

1 Draped design by Max.Tan S/S 2011.

**SOURCING AND SELECTING
TEXTILES FOR FASHION**

CHAPTER ONE: THE ROLE OF TEXTILES IN FASHION
CHAPTER TWO: MATERIALS
CHAPTER THREE: SURFACE DESIGN
CHAPTER FOUR: CONCEPTUALIZING THE COLLECTION
CHAPTER FIVE: SOURCING YOUR FABRIC
CHAPTER SIX: TEXTILES AND THE COLLECTION
SOURCING INTERVIEWS
APPENDIX

164

2

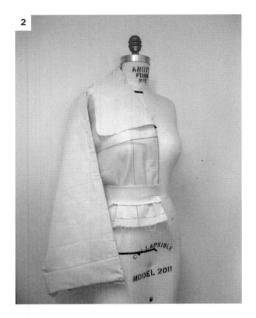

2 Start of a draped jacket on
the form. Courtesy of Professor
Karen Curinton-Perry.

Patternmaking

Patternmaking is an art form unto itself. Some designers excel at it and some are a bit more troubled. Many designers work in conjunction with a separate patternmaker to realize their designs. Either way it is important that a designer understands at least the rudimentary skills involved in patternmaking to be able to convey their ideas clearly at the patternmaking stage.

Patternmaking is a form of engineering. It requires the ability to visualize the transformation of an idea into a three-dimensional physical object. A patternmaker achieves this transformation through an understanding of the human form, textile properties, bodily proportions and construction methodology. Patternmaking expresses these understandings through the language of maths. It is important for a patternmaker to have a firm grasp on addition, subtraction, scale, curve, line and fractions.

Luckily, many books have been written on the subject of patternmaking, with clear instructions for patterning the most common fashion silhouettes and details like collars, sleeves and pockets. It is also easy to find a chart of the common body measurements needed to create flat patterns as they relate to fashion standard sizes. By using these standard instructions and charts as a starting point, a designer can manipulate and distort the standards to achieve their specific design goals.

The basic tools needed for patternmaking are rulers (one curve stick, one L-square), measuring tape, pencil, sharp paper scissors and roll paper. In addition there are specific tools made for patternmaking that are very helpful: pattern notch, tracing wheel, French curves, clear quilt ruler, awl and pattern punch. These tools can be sourced online or from most local sewing stores. When finished be sure to mark clearly the season, garment name and pattern piece on each pattern and hang all coordinating pieces together.

165

TEXTILE SELECTION AND GARMENT DESIGN
DRAWING YOUR DESIGNS
DRAPING AND PATTERNMAKING
PREPARING FOR PRODUCTION
EDITING THE COLLECTION
DESIGNER SPOTLIGHT – ISSEY MIYAKE

3

3 Fashion patterns can be plotted on various papers before the final production pattern is made.

Toile

Before moving forward into a final sample line each pattern must be checked for fit and function. This is done by constructing a toile, or prototype sample, in an inexpensive but similarly constructed textile to the final fashion garment. For a designer utilizing the paper pattern method this will be the first chance to see the garment design in a three-dimensional space. For a designer working with the draping process, the toile allows them to see if the drape was properly transferred to the paper pattern and has clear notation for accurate reassembly.

A toile is constructed using the same methods planned for the final garment including all sewn details. Often accessory closures will not be included but rather straight pins will substitute for buttons, snaps or zippers. A solid fabric is best as it allows for written notations and corrections to be marked legibly onto the toile. During the fitting it is advisable to move off the dress form and onto a live fit model. A fit model will exhibit the ideal body proportions of the brand's target customer. Observing the toile on a human body allows for better assessment of fit, movement, line and proportion.

**SOURCING AND SELECTING
TEXTILES FOR FASHION**

CHAPTER ONE: THE ROLE OF TEXTILES IN FASHION
CHAPTER TWO: MATERIALS
CHAPTER THREE: SURFACE DESIGN
CHAPTER FOUR: CONCEPTUALIZING THE COLLECTION
CHAPTER FIVE: SOURCING YOUR FABRIC
CHAPTER SIX: TEXTILES AND THE COLLECTION
SOURCING INTERVIEWS
APPENDIX

166

PREPARING FOR PRODUCTION

Now that the seasonal collection has been patterned and tested, it is time to move into final sample and production preparation. While some designers may construct the final sample line in studio, many send their patterns and fabrics out to a sample maker. Very few designers have the capability and facilities to handle production amounts and so production facilities will also need to be sourced.

In order to ensure a smooth transition from the designer's hand to the sample and production facilities it is a good idea to make sure each garment is accompanied by clear and precise instructions. Once these instructions have been received by the production house, a final cost estimate per garment will be sent to the designer. These numbers should be included in the final financial planning of the season's collection.

Flats

Flats are clear detailed renderings of the fashion garment. Unlike freehand fashion illustration, artistic flair is not as desirable in a flat as technical and proportionate accuracy to the final garment. Flats are drawn using a croquis as a guide to achieve correct proportion but they are not presented on a figure. Rather they describe how the garment would appear if laid flat on a surface. Both front and back of the garment and all details including seams, darts, stitching and trims must be included. Flats may be drawn by hand but CAD development of flats are becoming industry standard for spec sheets and technical packages. Computer aided design programmes using vector imagery allow for exact proportional scale and minute detailing. Hand rendering continues to be used often for animated flats. **Animated flats** indicate some movement and flair, making them nicer for line sheets, promotional packages and trend presentation.

Flats of the same garment will often be rendered twice: once in black-and-white detail, and a second with colour, textile and surface design filled in. Black-and-white flats are used for technical descriptions on spec sheets. In a **technical flat** various line weights are used to describe differing construction methods and design elements. Accurate stitch spacing and findings, trim and hardware placement must be recorded. **Coloured flats** will be used in a technical package to further describe textile and surface design placement. They will also be included in line sheet packages for buyers to show the various textile and surface options available in a given silhouette.

1 (opposite) After making fabric selections based on inspiration, customer and market the designer starts to conceptualize silhouette and collection. Hand-rendered flats courtesy of Anne Lysonski.

167

TEXTILE SELECTION AND GARMENT DESIGN
DRAWING YOUR DESIGNS
DRAPING AND PATTERNMAKING
PREPARING FOR PRODUCTION
EDITING THE COLLECTION
DESIGNER SPOTLIGHT – ISSEY MIYAKE

1

ribbon trim | Nylon mesh | Chiffon | Chiffon | Chiffon | Crepe back satin | Crepe back satin | Chiffon | Silk ribbon trim

Lace | Bow closure | ribbon trim | Lace

Bra and thong set
Lace and silk ribbon details

Bra and Panty set
Chiffon over crepe back satin
Lace trim

Corset with garter strings
Chiffon over crepe back satin
Ribbon detail

Romper nightgown
Sheer chiffon
Silk ribbon trim

Corset and thong set
Chiffon and Ribbon and bow trim
Ribbon thong

Nightgown
Sheer chiffon and lace bust

Nylon mesh stockings

SOURCING AND SELECTING
TEXTILES FOR FASHION

CHAPTER ONE: THE ROLE OF TEXTILES IN FASHION
CHAPTER TWO: MATERIALS
CHAPTER THREE: SURFACE DESIGN
CHAPTER FOUR: CONCEPTUALIZING THE COLLECTION
CHAPTER FIVE: SOURCING YOUR FABRIC
CHAPTER SIX: TEXTILES AND THE COLLECTION
SOURCING INTERVIEWS
APPENDIX

168

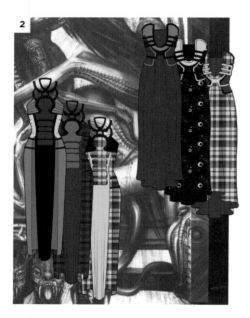

2 Computer programs make it easy to create detailed flats, which can then be coloured with a variety of different textile options. Courtesy of student Judy Yi.

Spec sheets and tech packages

Spec sheet is industry lingo for a specification sheet. A spec sheet will be included with each pattern and/or technical package submitted for garment construction. Included on the sheet will be a front and back technical flat of the garment, construction notes, a numbered list coordinating the flat to finished garment measurements, textile yardage needed, and trim and hardware details. A truncated spec sheet can be considered if it is accompanying a final pattern with supporting photographs or toile. However, if someone else is creating the pattern as well as sample and production they will need as much detailed information as possible.

When employing auxiliary contractors to handle the processes of patternmaking, first sample, final sample and production, a complete **technical package** should be assembled. All technical packages should be clearly labelled with designer name, season, year and garment name. A tech pack for a pattern and toile maker, in addition to a highly detailed spec sheet, should include photos or samples of any draping techniques or unusual construction details. Swatches or sample yardage of textiles can be included so the patternmaker has a clear understanding of the design vision and final textile properties. A chart with brand-specific measurements per size should be included as the patternmaker will need to grade the final pattern into a range of sizes, or a **grading nest**. Have toiles made up of each and every garment prior to signing off on its production pattern. If it is not affordable to have every garment sampled in each size, try to have at least one done to double check the grading. **Production patterns** will be made in a durable card stock to be used by the manufacturer of your line. Technical packages going to a final **sample maker** should include all of the above as well as yardage of textiles and trims, chosen hardware, coloured flats, the production pattern, the corrected toile and supporting photographs. A **sample line** of the collection can often be made by the final **production contractor**. This is a best case scenario because it helps ensure costly construction mistakes will be addressed and understood by the manufacturer prior to moving into production. The sample line is the collection of **final sample** garments showing exactly what the customer or buyer will receive from production orders.

When working with overseas vendors often only the creative and technical design of a garment is completed in-house. All other processes of garment construction including sourcing of materials, patternmaking, first and final samples, surface design processes and production will be handled by the overseas vendor. If the contact vendor does not have the ability to complete some aspects of the project, they will most likely take on the job of sourcing a local auxiliary contractor that can. When working overseas, flats, spec sheets and technical packages become extremely important for a smooth process and correct product.

169

TEXTILE SELECTION AND GARMENT DESIGN
DRAWING YOUR DESIGNS
DRAPING AND PATTERNMAKING
PREPARING FOR PRODUCTION
EDITING THE COLLECTION
DESIGNER SPOTLIGHT – ISSEY MIYAKE

Costing

Costing is the budgeting of fashion design. It takes into account production cost, wholesale price and retail price. In the end, the designer's understanding of the costing of a garment can have a direct impact on the overall success of their business. Poor costing calculations will sink a running business quicker than a poorly designed collection. Costing should be considered at every stage of the design process. A good designer must acknowledge its impact on textile selection and the designs themselves.

A good costing calculation will start with the projected retail price point of a designer's line. A designer should study target market, economic climate and competitors' prices to come up with a range of price points per garment category for their brand. Working backwards, a retailer will often mark up the **wholesale price** of a garment 2 to 2.5 times to achieve **retail price**. If a skirt will sell for £53.00 ($80.00) retail, then the wholesale price will be £21–26 ($32–40) depending on what type of pricing structure your retailer buyers employ. As a designer you will want to earn a **gross margin** of 50% over cost of garment, at £26 ($40) wholesale that leaves £13 ($20) which can be spent on designing and creating the garment. Understand that the 50% gross margin will not total what goes back into the business. What goes back into the business will be net profit. **Net profit** should be a projected 35%, no less. The spare 15% will help absorb sales rep fees, overstock, unpaid and cancelled orders.

There are a number of factors that go into the costing of the actual garment. Static costing variables will include salaries, rent, accounting fees and monthly bills. **Overhead** is the general term for these items and a rough calculation can be made by adding 30% of the variable cost totals. However, it is advisable to calculate as accurate a figure as possible. **Garment costs** include development and sampling, fabric and trim yields, labels, and all production labour costs. These are variable and the only part of the costing development that allow reduction adjustments to be made. When trying to reduce production costs on a fashion item, the designer must make sure quality, market level and retail price points do not suffer.

SOURCING AND SELECTING
TEXTILES FOR FASHION

CHAPTER ONE: THE ROLE OF TEXTILES IN FASHION
CHAPTER TWO: MATERIALS
CHAPTER THREE: SURFACE DESIGN
CHAPTER FOUR: CONCEPTUALIZING THE COLLECTION
CHAPTER FIVE: SOURCING YOUR FABRIC
CHAPTER SIX: TEXTILES AND THE COLLECTION
SOURCING INTERVIEWS
APPENDIX

170

EDITING THE COLLECTION

Armed with all the information gained through the development of a collection, the designer turns a critical eye to the final results. Never will a design collection move forward exactly as planned at the start of design development. Along the way there will be conceptual changes, material changes and surprise additions. Fashion design is a living organism that reacts to its environment as it grows. Editing happens throughout the design process, yet a final analysis of the line is necessary prior to moving forward into production. A wise designer trusts their instincts but takes others' feedback into consideration.

Design considerations

By the time the final sample line is assembled there have most likely already been many edits, cuts and changes to the collection. A first editing session will occur after all designs have been illustrated, a second during textile sourcing and third as garments are patterned and toiled. During these sessions editing may be as simple as combining two okay designs into one fabulous one, substituting a textile or changing a construction choice. The editing done during the final analysis will cut styles from the line entirely.

The final analysis of design considerations will occur in a two-part approach: one prior to the show or market week and one after, prior to production. Before a line is shown to the public it should be viewed in its entirety. The people viewing it should include not only the designer but also support staff and trusted business mentors. The final sample line should be viewed on live models and each garment evaluated for fit, function, garment aesthetics and flow within the line. Issues in any of these areas may not be apparent until the final sample is presented in the correct colour, textile and surface. If an issue is discovered at this late stage, the garment most likely will need to be scrapped or reworked for a future collection. After the show and market week a second analysis should be made based on press and buyer reactions. In every collection there will always be pieces that just do not resonate with the audience even if all design targets are being met. It is best to try to weed these items out prior to spending money on production.

171

TEXTILE SELECTION AND GARMENT DESIGN
DRAWING YOUR DESIGNS
DRAPING AND PATTERNMAKING
PREPARING FOR PRODUCTION
EDITING THE COLLECTION
DESIGNER SPOTLIGHT – ISSEY MIYAKE

1 M.Patmos collections focus on fair trade, sustainable materials and socially conscious production methods as well as design and colour trends. M. Patmos Knitwear S/S 2012.

Financial considerations

As discussed in the costing section of this chapter, there are times when finances play a role in the editing of a collection. As the collection is formed financial budgets will affect textile and material selections, surface design capabilities, design elements and construction methods. There are many financial variables to play with to achieve a balance between your design ethos and the budget. This can be achieved by editing design variables: for example a fabulous and expensive fabric can be married with a simpler design and cheaper construction costs or a simpler fabric with a more complicated design. Another financial editing trick is to fluctuate the gross profit margin (GPM) per item across the entire line. If a must-have item's production price will end in a way too high wholesale and retail price, a designer can take a lower profit margin and make it up by adding a higher GPM to a less expensive garment. Another variable to consider is appeal. If a garment is very popular ensuring high production orders, often times a lower production cost can be negotiated to keep it on the line.

There will be times, however, that an item, no matter how fabulous, does not make financial sense for production. If the design is solid it is worth exploring in the future with less expensive textiles, surface additions or simplified patterning. Occasionally a designer will move forward with a design knowing it will be too expensive for production. These 'runway pieces' make good financial sense as they will often garner a lot of press and attention for the collection.

Ultimately, no designer will ever be able to fully edit down to a winning collection every season. Hopefully this text has given an overview of the many ways to work textiles into a successful fashion line. Fashion is a moving target, arm yourself with as much knowledge as possible and fire away.

DESIGNER SPOTLIGHT
ISSEY MIYAKE

I have endeavoured to make fundamental changes to the system of making clothes. Think: a thread goes into a machine, that in turn generates complete clothing using the latest computer technology and eliminates the usual needs for cutting and sewing the fabric.
Issey Miyake

The works of few designers highlight the symbiotic relationship between textile and fashion design like Issey Miyake's. His fashion career is an exploratory marriage of technology, textile innovation and clean simple design. Often his work leaves one wondering where he started: with the cloth or with the design concept? Or if there really is a distinction between the two? Highly conceptual and often extremely tactile Miyake's design work engages both the body and the mind. By focusing on broad inspirations with philosophical implications he does not tie his aspirations to the preconceived notions of fashion design. One gets the feeling that the artistic journey is just as important as the beauty of the end result.

DISCUSSION QUESTIONS

1

Miyake recently retired from his position as Head of Design to focus on the construction and conception of the textiles used in his collections – do you think fashion and textile conception and fashion design are one and the same thing?

2

How do you build a collection? Do you design according to the textiles you source or do you source textiles for your design concepts? Would you be comfortable working either way?

3

Miyake Design Studio's head designer, Dai Fujiwara has said 'I do not believe that any discussion of art is possible without bringing technology onboard.' Do you find this to be true? Do you think this statement will be more relevant as we move into the future?

4

It has been said that Issey Miyake focuses on his craft for art's sake while many of his fashion peers focus on the bottom line. Do you think it is possible to focus on both high concept design and profitability at once? Is there room for many designers like Issey Miyake in the marketplace or do you feel he is an outlier?

5

What inspires you to push the boundaries of design concept?

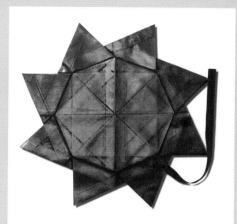

Creations from Issey Miyake's
132 5 collection.

Sourcing Interviews

Textile selection can be as important to the success of a fashion line as the designs themselves. Being able to analyse properly your customer's needs, what you can afford, and what textile properties your designs require, will allow you to more successfully source the perfect fabric. Being aware of custom construction methods, colouring and surface design options allows more freedom for the creation of the textiles you are unable to source. The following interviews offer a glimpse at how some designers studying and working in the industry source or create their textiles. These stories told by designers at different stages of their careers and working in various markets are meant to inspire and guide you in your own line creation.

SOURCING AND SELECTING
TEXTILES FOR FASHION

CHAPTER ONE: THE ROLE OF TEXTILES IN FASHION
CHAPTER TWO: MATERIALS
CHAPTER THREE: SURFACE DESIGN
CHAPTER FOUR: CONCEPTUALIZING THE COLLECTION
CHAPTER FIVE: SOURCING YOUR FABRIC
CHAPTER SIX: TEXTILES AND THE COLLECTION
SOURCING INTERVIEWS
APPENDIX

176

STUDENT DESIGNER

THERESA DECKNER

Theresa Deckner was completing her senior thesis collection for Pratt Institute in Brooklyn, NY at the time of this interview.

Do you customize your own fabrics through surface design? Yes, I love painting and dyeing my own fabrics. I like experimenting both with different techniques and also using initial paintings or drawings to create textile patterns on Adobe Photoshop and Adobe Illustrator.

What processes do you work with for this? It is difficult to narrow down processes as I am constantly trying out new and different things. For my senior collection I used a mix of acrylic paint and a polymer emulsion from Golden (GAC 900) to colour wash/paint the hemp and hemp blend fabrics I used. The polymer emulsion makes the painted fabrics washable/colour fast and able to retain its original hand compared to a very stiffened fabric if only using acrylics.

Do you have any special interests that affect fabric selection? Right now I am extremely interested in using and sourcing hemp fabrics. It is an incredibly versatile fabric that has low impact on the environment. Unfortunately it is not legally manufactured in most countries and somewhat difficult to come by without long-distance shipping.

What is the most important quality you look for in a textile? I am not very utilitarian in the way I choose my fabrics. I often get distracted by the way fabrics feel instead of being strict about function. I love soft and airy materials that drape well and feel good on the skin. However, any material has to serve a specific purpose and I do try to use that as the starting point of any fabric decision. I also try to make the best decision possible based on how much impact my fabric choice will have on the environment.

Do you design and then look for textiles to work with your designs or do you source a selection of fabrics then design to them? I usually design, and then look for fabrics to work with. The fabrics have to accommodate a specific function for each individual piece of clothing so, to me, most of the time choosing the right fabric is the second step. However there are times when a really amazing print or colour or the way a fabric feels (mostly cashmeres) get me excited to draw or start making clothes.

How important is colour in your collection? Colour is extremely important because it is usually what inspires any of my designs initially. For this specific collection I was inspired by flowers I had seen on several hikes around Germany where I had spent some time last summer. After returning to New York I used pictures I had taken to make different colour boards until I had found the combination I liked the most.

177

STUDENT DESIGNER
JUST STARTING OUT
INDIE CONTEMPORARY DESIGNER
SUSTAINABLE DESIGNER
MASS-MARKET DESIGNER
STREETWEAR DESIGNER
WOMENSWEAR DESIGNER
TEXTILE DESIGNER
DIGITAL CUSTOMIZATION

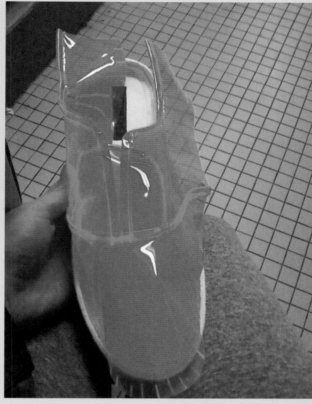

How important is surface design in your collection?
Surface design is what defines this collection the
most to me. I love painting but have always been
somewhat insecure and private about it. I usually
paint when I feel overwhelmed. To me each part of
any of my paintings or drawings means something
specific to me. This collection was really important to
me in that it was the first time I combined painting/
putting my thoughts into colour and making clothes –
for people to actually see – out of them.

**Do you feel like your designs are known for your
fabric selection or surface design additions?** I would
expect them to be known for both fabric selection
and surface design.

**SOURCING AND SELECTING
TEXTILES FOR FASHION**

CHAPTER ONE: THE ROLE OF TEXTILES IN FASHION
CHAPTER TWO: MATERIALS
CHAPTER THREE: SURFACE DESIGN
CHAPTER FOUR: CONCEPTUALIZING THE COLLECTION
CHAPTER FIVE: SOURCING YOUR FABRIC
CHAPTER SIX: TEXTILES AND THE COLLECTION
SOURCING INTERVIEWS
APPENDIX

178

JUST STARTING OUT

KELSY CARLEEN PARKHOUSE

Kelsy Carleen Parkhouse is a recent fashion design graduate of Pratt Institute 2012. Her senior collection was awarded the inaugural Liz Claiborne Award – Concept to Product grant to help cover the costs of developing a collection to show during New York Fashion Week. The first collection of her new line, Carleen, debuting at S/S 2013 Fashion Week will be an extension of her senior thesis work. Her work is inspired by vintage, craft and collectibles and growing up on the West Coast. <www.carleen.us>

How long have you been designing? I recently graduated from school and started my own company, Carleen. I've been designing for about four years.

What are the challenges of textile selection for your product? One of the biggest challenges so far has simply been sourcing wholesale vendors for the first time and meeting order minimums. I'm hoping this will get easier as I get more established and continue to gain experience.

What kind of outlets do you tend to source from? I started my first collection while in school and with more limited resources. I wanted to use a lot of prints, so I turned to vintage textiles that I source through eBay. Since then I have also turned to mills and creating custom prints.

Do you work with established business connections season to season or source new vendors depending on collection? As a new independent designer, sourcing vendors has been a challenge. Contacts from former jobs and internships have been very useful, but I am looking forward to building relationships with vendors I can count on.

Do you customize your own fabrics through surface design? It depends on what the collection calls for, it isn't something I plan on doing consistently across seasons. For my senior thesis I utilized quilting, patchwork and silkscreen. In the future I'd like to explore embroidery and dyeing techniques.

Do you have any special interests that affect fabric selection? I am interested in sustainability and local industry, but it is not a primary focus of my company or my brand. I try to make good choices whenever possible.

What is the most important quality you look for in a textile? Is 'all of the above' an acceptable answer? Different qualities take on more importance depending on the particular project, but texture and hand are high on the list. Finding the right shade of a particular colour is also pretty important.

Do you design and then look for textiles to work with your designs or do you source a selection of fabrics then design to them? It's more common for me to design first and go back for textiles, but there have been instances where one fabric will be really inspiring and inform a large portion of the collection.

How important is colour in your collection? Very important! Choosing a colour palette usually happens pretty early in my design process.

Do you feel like your designs are known for your fabric selection or surface design additions? The patchwork and quilting I am using for my Spring 13 collection have been receiving a lot of attention since our senior fashion show. It's too soon to tell if it'll be an element that people continue to associate with my work.

179

STUDENT DESIGNER
JUST STARTING OUT
INDIE CONTEMPORARY DESIGNER
SUSTAINABLE DESIGNER
MASS-MARKET DESIGNER
STREETWEAR DESIGNER
WOMENSWEAR DESIGNER
TEXTILE DESIGNER
DIGITAL CUSTOMIZATION

SOURCING AND SELECTING
TEXTILES FOR FASHION

CHAPTER ONE: THE ROLE OF TEXTILES IN FASHION
CHAPTER TWO: MATERIALS
CHAPTER THREE: SURFACE DESIGN
CHAPTER FOUR: CONCEPTUALIZING THE COLLECTION
CHAPTER FIVE: SOURCING YOUR FABRIC
CHAPTER SIX: TEXTILES AND THE COLLECTION
SOURCING INTERVIEWS
APPENDIX

180

INDIE CONTEMPORARY DESIGNER
DAVID J. KRAUSE AND NINA ZILKA FOR ALDER

Alder is the second line for designers David J. Krause and Nina Zilka. Their first line, the twentyten, was a success from the launch while still students and featured in *Surface Magazine*, Refinery 29, *WWD* and *Elle*. It remained successful until 2011 when they closed it to move creatively in a different direction. The new line, Alder, is minimalist and essential while remaining playful.

What are your job title and responsibilities? I'm the co-owner and designer of Alder. I, along with my business partner, Nina Zilka, am responsible for every aspect of running a fashion label. Some responsibilities include patternmaking, sample sewing, production management, sales, PR and marketing.

How long have you been designing? I've been designing since 2008 when I formed my first clothing label, the twentyten.

Describe your line. Alder is a clothing, accessories and natural hair care company that focuses on creating quality products that are responsibly and locally made. Alder additionally crafts goods that have unique details that our customers cherish.

What kind of outlets do you tend to source from? We source our textiles directly from mills and textile showrooms.

Do you work with established business connections season to season or source new vendors depending on collection? We work with a group of different textile showrooms and mills season to season. We also source new businesses out each season when looking for a specific textile or fibre.

Do you customize your own fabrics through surface design? We often create custom digital prints, screened prints and dye effects each season.

Do you create/design your fabrics in-house, outsource freelance or buy from market? We create all our custom textiles in-house. We also purchase textiles as is from the market.

Do you do in-house trend research? Yes, we do all of our own trend research.

How many seasons ahead do you work? We work up to two years ahead of a season.

Do you have any special interests that affect fabric selection? We try to source fabrics as locally when possible. However, quality is the main focus. Creating long lasting, well-made products is the most important factor in our fabric selection.

Do you design and then look for textiles to work with your designs or do you source a selection of fabrics then design to them? We often design a collection with some ideas of what colours or fibres we would like to use. We then try sourcing the fabrics we envisioned and then revise our designs depending on what we find. We then decide on what textiles and fabric treatments we will be creating to complement our already selected fabrics.

How important is colour in your collection? Colour is extremely important to our collections. Often colour is the unifying element for a season.

SOURCING AND SELECTING
TEXTILES FOR FASHION

CHAPTER ONE: THE ROLE OF TEXTILES IN FASHION
CHAPTER TWO: MATERIALS
CHAPTER THREE: SURFACE DESIGN
CHAPTER FOUR: CONCEPTUALIZING THE COLLECTION
CHAPTER FIVE: SOURCING YOUR FABRIC
CHAPTER SIX: TEXTILES AND THE COLLECTION
SOURCING INTERVIEWS
APPENDIX

182

SUSTAINABLE DESIGNER

JOHN PATRICK FOR JOHN PATRICK ORGANIC

John Patrick designed in the New York City fashion industry for 20 years before deciding to scrap that lifestyle for a chance to go green. It took four years of dedicated research and planning but in 2006 John Patrick Organics was born. The line is a perfect blend of luxury, detail-driven design and ethics. Based on innovative, fair trade textile sourcing locally and abroad, the line focuses on traditional practices married to advances in botanical dyes, digital print techniques, recycled fabrics and organic wool yarns.

What is your job title? Head zoo keeper – head designer of all design and fabrications

Who is your target market? We seem to have a wide range – as a contemporary fashion brand our target would be a contemporary fashion customer.

What are the challenges of textile selection for your brand? The challenges are that the fabric mills are very unwilling to innovate in the USA. The leadership in textiles for my brand comes from Japan.

What kind of outlets do you tend to source from? I work with small to medium to large mills. I am always on the lookout for new and innovative suppliers.

Do you customize your own fabrics through colour or print? What processes do you work with for this? We do. Digital print has been introduced since 2008.

What are specialized concerns for textile selection for your market? Authenticity – transparency and sustainability are the hallmarks of the brand.

Is global sourcing part of how you find textiles? Yes. We are very selective and work only with firms we know.

Do you do in-house trend research? How many seasons ahead do you work? We do not follow any trends. We work on each collection six months ahead.

What is the importance of textiles in your design process? The textiles are the most important part of the collection after the design. They go hand-in-hand. If they are not unified there is no collection.

Do you source your seasonal textiles first and design to them or do you decide on design and then source the correct textile? Half and half. There are always surprises. It is sometimes quite accidental that a fabric works in an extraordinary way that was not expected.

Do you design surface treatments in-house? Yes, my studio does.

SOURCING AND SELECTING
TEXTILES FOR FASHION

CHAPTER ONE: THE ROLE OF TEXTILES IN FASHION
CHAPTER TWO: MATERIALS
CHAPTER THREE: SURFACE DESIGN
CHAPTER FOUR: CONCEPTUALIZING THE COLLECTION
CHAPTER FIVE: SOURCING YOUR FABRIC
CHAPTER SIX: TEXTILES AND THE COLLECTION
SOURCING INTERVIEWS
APPENDIX

184

MASS-MARKET DESIGNER

The designer for this mass-market interview agreed to share her experience anonymously due to non-disclosure agreements* in her past contracts. She graduated top of her fashion design class and has worked in the industry for 11 years. In that time she has held several positions with a large box chain store including technical designer and head designer for juniors. Recently she left her job as designer for a well-known fast fashion junior's line to help launch a new brand.

What are your job title and responsibilities? Design Director. I manage all aspects of design from concept development, to fabric and colour, style development, costing, to final product.

How long have you been designing? Ten years.

Who the brand's target market? Juniors fast fashion age 14–24.

Describe the brand you design for? Fast fashion juniors apparel. Cut & sew knits, wovens, denim and sweaters.

What are the challenges of textile selection for your product? Speed to market is the biggest challenge in fast fashion. Fabrics have long lead times. We try to buy greige in certain knits in advance, dyeing and designing closer to delivery in order to turn trend-right product quickly. Also we buy from vendors' existing fabrications instead of having them develop something from scratch.

What kind of outlets do you tend to source from? Most factories will source fabric and trims for you in larger quantities. They are also able to find minimum quantities or bolts of fabric occasionally to purchase at a slightly higher price per yard so that you can avoid the standard minimums.

Do you work with established business connections season to season or source new vendors depending on collection? The product drives what vendors you need to work with. Certain countries specialize in certain fabrics, trims or styles. For example India focuses primarily on wovens where China is the current leader in knits.

Do you customize your own fabrics through surface design? At large companies all prints and graphics are custom. There are graphic design teams that work with the designer closely to interpret the trends into brand right prints. They are experts in print application, though the designer is also responsible to know which prints may work best on certain fabrications.

How many seasons ahead do you work? In retail most trends are developed 9–12 months in advance, while the silhouette may be developed 6–9 months in advance. Prints are generally developed around the same time as the silhouettes. In fast fashion this timeline can be condensed to as little as 3–6 months for the entire process.

185

STUDENT DESIGNER
JUST STARTING OUT
INDIE CONTEMPORARY DESIGNER
SUSTAINABLE DESIGNER
MASS-MARKET DESIGNER
STREETWEAR DESIGNER
WOMENSWEAR DESIGNER
TEXTILE DESIGNER
DIGITAL CUSTOMIZATION

What is the most important quality you look for in a textile? Colour and hand is always the most important to maintain the brand integrity. Drape or structure is completely dependent on the end silhouette.

Do you have any advice you would like to give students on the importance of textile selection for a collection? Textile selection is extremely important. It separates great designers from good. To be a great designer you must know fabrics. It is your medium and without the knowledge it is impossible to design functional and beautiful product.

*A non-disclosure agreement is when you sign a contract with your employer. You are then unable to speak about or show your work, as the work belongs to the company. They are a common contractual agreement in the world of big business fashion.

SOURCING AND SELECTING
TEXTILES FOR FASHION

CHAPTER ONE: THE ROLE OF TEXTILES IN FASHION
CHAPTER TWO: MATERIALS
CHAPTER THREE: SURFACE DESIGN
CHAPTER FOUR: CONCEPTUALIZING THE COLLECTION
CHAPTER FIVE: SOURCING YOUR FABRIC
CHAPTER SIX: TEXTILES AND THE COLLECTION
SOURCING INTERVIEWS
APPENDIX

186

STREETWEAR DESIGNER

PHILIPPA PRICE AND SMILEY STEVENS FOR G.G.$

G.G.$. (Guns. Germs. Steal.) is a men's streetwear collection out of Los Angeles. Focusing on 'verge culture', the founders and designers, Philippa Price and Smiley Stevens work worldwide and turn high-end influences into wearable clothing with street cred. Their line combines spot and all-over prints with textured fabrics appealing to a new generation of urban and authentic men.

What are your job titles and responsibilities?
Philippa Price and Smiley Stevens are the co-founders and creative directors of G.G.$. We design the clothing and accessories, handle the branding, and oversee all aspects of our brand.

Who is your target market? Our target market is the new kind of emerging streetwear consumers who are influenced by more than skating and the streets – they are a part of 'verge culture', a fast expanding, multiracial subculture of millions, guided by an infinite flow of cultural influences. This new streetwear consumer grew up in a world that is highly designed and highly connected; he is no longer isolated in his experience of the typical environment of urban/street culture. He has developed an appreciation for fashion and tasteful design; and his personal style therefore has completely evolved.

Describe your line. Guns Germs $teal is a streetwear inspired men's brand with a diverse set of style influences. We sell men's accessories, graphic tees and cut-and-sew collections. Our cut-and-sew collections blend the functionality of classic workwear with the bold edge of streetwear style, all the while taking cues from high fashion movements.

What are the challenges of textile selection for your product? The main challenge is sourcing fabrics that you can be sure you will be able to reorder when it's time for production. We weren't fully aware of this when we designed our first collection ... so we created all of our samples, sold the line, but then when it came time for production we had to go back and order fabrics for production – it was a disaster.

What kind of outlets do you tend to source from?
When we're designing a collection, we start by going to a fabric trade show. We like to walk around and be surprised by what we find. Looking at fabrics is usually where we start designing a collection rather than designing the pieces first. Once we've got a good feel for what our collection will look like, we can go directly to mills around LA to source specific textiles. We have started to create a few prints ourselves, but again this becomes difficult and expensive in production, as you usually have to meet pretty high minimums.

Do you work with established business connections season to season or source new vendors depending on collection? Our vendors are constantly changing depending on the collection. We meet most new vendors at trade shows or by word-of-mouth. However, we tend to use established connections for more basic textiles and fabrics. We are still such a new brand we are still learning who and what are reliable sources.

**SOURCING AND SELECTING
TEXTILES FOR FASHION**

CHAPTER ONE: THE ROLE OF TEXTILES IN FASHION
CHAPTER TWO: MATERIALS
CHAPTER THREE: SURFACE DESIGN
CHAPTER FOUR: CONCEPTUALIZING THE COLLECTION
CHAPTER FIVE: SOURCING YOUR FABRIC
CHAPTER SIX: TEXTILES AND THE COLLECTION
SOURCING INTERVIEWS
APPENDIX

188

STREETWEAR DESIGNER

PHILIPPA PRICE AND SMILEY STEVENS FOR G.G.$

What processes do you work with for this? We are open to exploring all of these processes. We used a lot of sublimation and all-over print in our first line. This season we are using dip dye for some pieces, and we always use silk screening for our graphic tees. There are so many awesome technologies coming out with fabric printing and dyeing … it's exciting to keep discovering new ones as it opens up so many possibilities for textiles.

Do you create/design your fabrics in-house, outsource freelance or buy from market? We buy fabrics from the market and design some of our own. As we continue to grow, we definitely want to focus more on designing our own fabrics in-house.

What are specialized concerns for textile selection for your market? Our market is definitely drawn to graphics, but we're more concerned with introducing new textiles and prints to our market that they haven't seen before. We are definitely coming at men's streetwear from a completely new angle than most of the brands in our market, which I think allows us to be completely open minded when it comes to choosing fabrics.

How many people work towards textile selection and creation? Just Philippa and Smiley!

Do you do in-house trend research? We're constantly observing and doing our own personal research on emerging trends, but we try to stay ahead of them. Just from attending fabric shows, which are almost a year ahead of the seasons, you can tell what is going to be in over the upcoming year and we try to make sure we are NOT doing that. This past year ikat fabric was ALL over the fabric show … we loved some of the prints but we know by next spring season, every brand is going to be selling ikat fabric so we stayed clear of it. A fabric vendor tried to show us a 'trend forecast' once and we had to shield our eyes – we both feel that those things can be detrimental to your creativity.

How many seasons ahead do you work? Currently, we design just one season ahead. Right now we're coming up on our second season, we're still trying to keep up!

189

STUDENT DESIGNER
JUST STARTING OUT
INDIE CONTEMPORARY DESIGNER
SUSTAINABLE DESIGNER
MASS-MARKET DESIGNER
STREETWEAR DESIGNER
WOMENSWEAR DESIGNER
TEXTILE DESIGNER
DIGITAL CUSTOMIZATION

Do you have any special interests that affect fabric selection? Sourcing local fabrics is definitely important to us. Because we produce entirely in downtown LA, we save a lot of money by sourcing locally. Looking at it from an environmental perspective, finding our fabrics near where we produce lowers our carbon footprint.

What is the most important quality you look for in a textile? The print or colour.

Do you design and then look for textiles to work with your designs or do you source a selection of fabrics then design to them? We usually source a selection of fabrics and design to them.

How important is colour in your collection? Are you kidding me? The MOST important! Our collection designs start entirely with colour.

Do you have any advice you would like to give students on the importance of textile selection for a collection? BE ORGANIZED IN YOUR TEXTILE SELECTION, especially if you will be mass-producing the line. Nothing sucks more than having an amazing swatch and having no idea where you got it or creating a sample, selling it to stores, and then finding out when you go into production that the fabric is no longer available. Staple swatches to business cards, keep receipts and invoices, and before you get attached to a fabric, make sure you can actually order it wholesale and make sure the pricing makes sense with your line.

SOURCING AND SELECTING
TEXTILES FOR FASHION

CHAPTER ONE: THE ROLE OF TEXTILES IN FASHION
CHAPTER TWO: MATERIALS
CHAPTER THREE: SURFACE DESIGN
CHAPTER FOUR: CONCEPTUALIZING THE COLLECTION
CHAPTER FIVE: SOURCING YOUR FABRIC
CHAPTER SIX: TEXTILES AND THE COLLECTION
SOURCING INTERVIEWS
APPENDIX

190

WOMENSWEAR DESIGNER

TATA AND NAKA SURGULADZE FOR TATA NAKA/STOLEN MEMORIES

Tata Naka and Stolen Memories are two lines of one brand, owned and operated by the Georgia-born British twin sisters – Tamara and Natasha Surguladze. They are three-times recipients of The British Fashion Council's New Generations Award. The designers attended Central Saint Martins in London for fashion design producing press worthy, individual, final collections. After graduating they decided to form a family company, as is the custom in their home country. Tata Naka is a combined vision, adventurous, fun and stylish. <www.tatanaka.com>

What are your job titles and responsibilities? We are joint creative directors of Tata Naka. Our responsibilities include full creative control of the Tata Naka, Stolen Memories and TNTEES labels, designing and producing six collections a year. We are also involved in all aspects of the business from the production to the PR to the sales. It is a small company so we are very hands on!

How long have you been designing? Tata Naka was founded in 2000, launched from our respective graduate collections but we have been designing since we were children.

Who is your target market? Our target market is women who are stylish but not slaves to trends. An individual with a sense of humour and fun, who is adventurous and knows her own mind!

Describe your line. We do two main collections a year and two pre-collections under the Tata Naka label, which is itself split into Tata Naka and Stolen Memories reflecting the two designers who create it. We also have a contemporary line which launched in AW12 called TNTEEs which is timed to come out with pre-collections for the main line.

What are the challenges of textile selection for your product? We are a small company so we are always constrained by cost as a factor. A lot of the mills and fabric suppliers have very high minimums so we are limited in our choices in the first place. Secondly a lot of the fabric distributors will push you to sample with a certain mill or fabric without checking and ensuring that said fabric will be readily available for production – this happens a lot and results in scouring the country to find a match for some material that you are now committed to producing 150 pieces with! Thirdly, and most importantly, there is no money to invest in R&D, that is in developing fabrics that will work better for the designer, which would really be something we would love to explore but this only happens with major sponsorship.

What kind of outlets do you tend to source from? We source from mills and through distributors. We also create textiles ourselves – prints, embroideries, trims, etc.

Do you customize your own fabrics through surface design? Yes.

What processes do you work with for this? Digital print, placement, all over, appliqué, beading, etc.

191

STUDENT DESIGNER
JUST STARTING OUT
INDIE CONTEMPORARY DESIGNER
SUSTAINABLE DESIGNER
MASS-MARKET DESIGNER
STREETWEAR DESIGNER
WOMENSWEAR DESIGNER
TEXTILE DESIGNER
DIGITAL CUSTOMIZATION

Do you create/design your fabrics in-house, outsource freelance or buy from market? We create in-house – all our prints start as either paintings or drawings or sculpture created by the designers and then converted digitally. We also use photography as a medium to create our own prints. Our jacquards are also woven to our specifications to include designs done by us.

Do you design and then look for textiles to work with your designs or do you source a selection of fabrics then design to them? Yes we have an idea of the type of fabric we are looking for, for each design, so in the majority of cases the design comes first. However sometimes when we are sourcing we will see a particular textile that we love and we then create a design to match it.

How important is colour in your collection? As print is a big part of our work, colour is very important to Tata Naka. Colour not just for prints but also the range of solid colours that we use in every collection and how we mix them with other textiles as accents. Our best seller this last season was a colour-blocked tweed biker coat and jacket featuring five different colours mixed with other textiles as accents.

SOURCING AND SELECTING
TEXTILES FOR FASHION

CHAPTER ONE: THE ROLE OF TEXTILES IN FASHION
CHAPTER TWO: MATERIALS
CHAPTER THREE: SURFACE DESIGN
CHAPTER FOUR: CONCEPTUALIZING THE COLLECTION
CHAPTER FIVE: SOURCING YOUR FABRIC
CHAPTER SIX: TEXTILES AND THE COLLECTION
SOURCING INTERVIEWS
APPENDIX

192

TEXTILE DESIGNER

ASTRID FARRUGGIA, LE STUDIO ANTHOST

Le Studio Anthost, opened in 2000, is one of the few ateliers in the US that produce painted fabrics using traditional couturier and highly sophisticated new techniques. Photos, antique prints, architecture and nature influence the studio's creations. Products are developed in New York and no machines are used, starting from making the screens to printing the fabrics. <www.lestudioanthost.com>

How did you decide on this career path? It was back when I was 23 years old...I had just graduated from an interior design school and found myself looking for, and finding, a job that I did not like. I had the chance and opportunity to meet two great people, Alexandre and Celine (husband and wife), who owned Atelier Dynale in France, a textile design studio working for haute couture designers such as Lacroix, Givenchy, Dior, Jean Paul Gaultier, and many more. They were my mentors. For two years they taught me the classic artisan craftsmanship of embellishments that Fortuny had developed, as well as many other techniques. It was an amazing experience to learn such a high level of detail and beautiful work, and to be taught by one of the few artisans who still exist. From this amazing experience, I decided that I wanted to go into textile design.

You work with very high-end and well-known designers. How did this start? A few years after moving to New York, I started promoting the Atelier Dynale. Selling beautiful work was a great way to get to know designers and it was easy to promote the Atelier Dynale; their skills were so amazing, the work spoke for itself. Unfortunately, it didn't work out as I had hoped because their classical craftsmanship was at such a high-end level, and it was hard to adapt to the American market. However, one of the designers I had contacted approached me about creating something for one of their collections. It didn't appear hard to accomplish. I set up a table in my living room, and started. It worked out well, so I

called all the designers that I had contacted earlier and they wanted to work with me. At the time, the classic techniques of fabric embellishment had not existed in the US. This provided me with a great opportunity to start Le Studio Anthost.

Do you follow any trends when looking to start a new textile line? I used to follow the trends, but I find it blocks the imagination. My specialty is to use what I have learned from the classical techniques in innovative ways to suite my clients' different tastes and needs. I have a more one-on-one relationship with each of the designers I work with, so the pieces I develop are according to their inspirations and themes.

What has been your favourite collaboration? My favourite collaboration is with the head designer of Carolina Herrera. Besides our French connection, he has a similar design aesthetic and comes from the same classical haute couture school as myself. Because of this I understand his tastes very well and it is easy for me to translate his ideas into works of art.

What is your favourite surface treatment or textile you have created? There are so many techniques that I love to work with, but the one I like to use the most is airbrushing. It gives a subtle, airy, light and whimsical feel to the fabric. It is also an alternative to printing and, if used correctly, there are many different ways to achieve unique looks. I especially love this technique when it influences the fabric to give a beautiful photographic appearance.

193

STUDENT DESIGNER
JUST STARTING OUT
INDIE CONTEMPORARY DESIGNER
SUSTAINABLE DESIGNER
MASS-MARKET DESIGNER
STREETWEAR DESIGNER
WOMENSWEAR DESIGNER
TEXTILE DESIGNER
DIGITAL CUSTOMIZATION

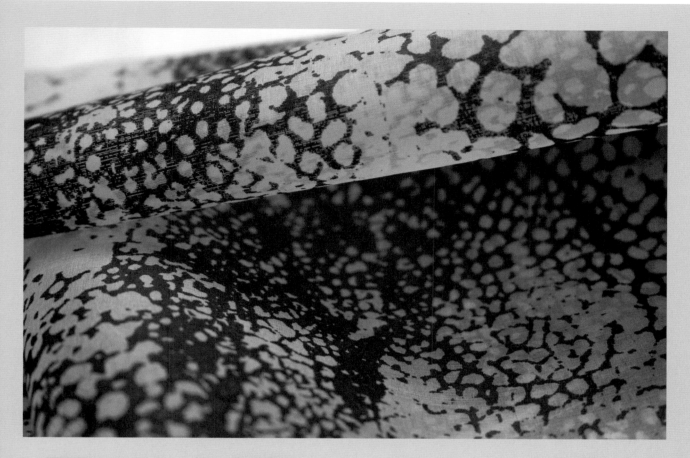

SOURCING AND SELECTING
TEXTILES FOR FASHION

CHAPTER ONE: THE ROLE OF TEXTILES IN FASHION
CHAPTER TWO: MATERIALS
CHAPTER THREE: SURFACE DESIGN
CHAPTER FOUR: CONCEPTUALIZING THE COLLECTION
CHAPTER FIVE: SOURCING YOUR FABRIC
CHAPTER SIX: TEXTILES AND THE COLLECTION
SOURCING INTERVIEWS
APPENDIX

194

TEXTILE DESIGNER

ASTRID FARRUGGIA, LE STUDIO ANTHOST

What process do you really enjoy? I really enjoy the sample development part. Especially when a designer pushes me to a level of creativity that is mind-blowing...this is when I usually develop new techniques.

How do you source your base fabrics? The designers supply most of the fabrics I work with.

How many seasons ahead do you work? One season, and it is more than enough!

Are all processes done by hand in your studio? Yes everything is done by hand...from beginning to end.

Do you ever contract out? How did you find vendors to work with up to your standards?

I thought about contracting out, but there is a certain beauty achieved in a piece that is absolutely one of a kind. This is what we are known for, so it would go against what Le Studio Anthost is about. Besides, I don't think the designers would appreciate it if the work was done outside. They come to me for something special, done locally, and by hand...they want the 'Le Studio hand'.

However, I am thinking of collaborating with digital printers, in which I would create an original piece and work with the designer to develop from that a digital print.

Do you only create the initial textile for the fashion sample and couture piece? Can your work be translated into production? How? I create the initial sample and couture piece as well as their production. My studio is capable of producing large amounts up to 457.2 m (500 yd) per a given order. In some cases when a production can be translated into a digital print, we might only work on the sample piece. It depends on what the designer wants. However, most of the techniques we develop can only be done in-house because of their special nature.

How important is colour to your work? Colour is extremely important to me. It is one of the few things that drive me. If I had not chosen this career, I think I would have been a colourist.

An important part of textile design is doing colour research. For me, it is exhilarating when a designer gives a tiny colour swatch and through careful and precise calculations I can match the exact colour in every different type of lighting and ground. The process of defining the chemistry of a colour, to find a recipe that can be used over and over is similar to working in a laboratory. The challenge motivates me, and provides an incredible sense of satisfaction and achievement when I can accomplish a successful colour match. The process is very exact, and the more I do it, the more I appreciate and understand about colour.

How many textile samples will you make before moving forward with a new process? My relationship with the designers I work with is so one-on-one that I basically have to be in their head, understanding their own personal tastes, to achieve something I know they would like. This process takes research, and I could have anything from 10 to 30 samples made for a designer before I even get the job. These are usually the first set of samples that are then narrowed down to one or two that pushes me in the right direction. The last pieces are usually the best.

Where does the process of design start for you? There is never really a start. Inspiration for design is continuously happening. I might see something around me that ignites inspiration to create. It is very exciting; there is a world of possibilities that can push you to develop ideas into great pieces.

195

STUDENT DESIGNER
JUST STARTING OUT
INDIE CONTEMPORARY DESIGNER
SUSTAINABLE DESIGNER
MASS-MARKET DESIGNER
STREETWEAR DESIGNER
WOMENSWEAR DESIGNER
TEXTILE DESIGNER
DIGITAL CUSTOMIZATION

SOURCING AND SELECTING
TEXTILES FOR FASHION

CHAPTER ONE: THE ROLE OF TEXTILES IN FASHION
CHAPTER TWO: MATERIALS
CHAPTER THREE: SURFACE DESIGN
CHAPTER FOUR: CONCEPTUALIZING THE COLLECTION
CHAPTER FIVE: SOURCING YOUR FABRIC
CHAPTER SIX: TEXTILES AND THE COLLECTION
SOURCING INTERVIEWS
APPENDIX

196

DIGITAL CUSTOMIZATION

YELENA KONOVALOVA, OWNER OF EYE DAZZLER STUDIO / HANNAH ROSS, STUDENT INTERN

Eye Dazzler is an independent textile design studio employing a team of international designers. The studio focuses on the creation of original and innovative print artwork aimed at the fashion and home markets. The studio was founded in 2009 by Erik Lisard and Yelena Konovalova and now has two studio locations in Brookyn, New York and Dalston, London.

YELENA KONOVALOVA

When a fashion designer purchases one of your designs does it become exclusive to their line?
All Eye Dazzler prints are one-of-a-kind. Fashion designers purchasing our artwork acquire the exclusive right to its use by default. Under no circumstance do we sell the same print twice. We relinquish creative control for all prints sold, and impose no limitations over how they are used. Once a client has the print, they can run with it as is or tailor its fine details to suit their current season.

Does your studio work with designers to create custom prints specific to their vision? Is this more expensive than purchasing off your line?
We regularly have designers coming to us with an idea they would like us to develop. Sometimes it is very specific and other times it is very vague – perhaps simply a mood they would like to recreate. It is an exciting process that presents its own set of challenges. There is often a different creative approach required in developing custom prints, depending on the situation. We need to understand more specifically the brand's customer, their sensibility, and the way they use prints in the clothes they design. We will happily develop any concept for a designer, usually creating a selection of five or six designs for them to choose from. We charge the same price for a custom print as we would for a print from our regular collection.

What do you see as the advantages of digital print for a fashion designer over traditional print methods? With digital printing comes more flexibility. Almost any image can be recreated digitally, whether it is a photograph, a painting or a gradient that calls for delicate tonal transitions. We can print in a wide array of colours and more easily create depth and atmosphere. It also streamlines the process of production, cutting out the need to separate colours and permitting for last-minute changes to the design. In short, it allows for vast creative freedom with very few restrictions, and that could bring a fashion designer much closer to fulfilling his or her vision.

Do you have any advice or suggestions for an emerging fashion designer hoping to add digital prints to their collection? Digital printing introduces endless possibilities, and in that sense it is as freeing as it is dangerous. Print is a powerful method of expression and you must find a good relationship between your sense of fashion design and your print choices. It is important to identify the strengths of digital printing and use it to its maximum, be bold and open minded about what is possible. All elements should be necessary and, as with all design, sometimes less can be more!

197

STUDENT DESIGNER
JUST STARTING OUT
INDIE CONTEMPORARY DESIGNER
SUSTAINABLE DESIGNER
MASS-MARKET DESIGNER
STREETWEAR DESIGNER
WOMENSWEAR DESIGNER
TEXTILE DESIGNER
DIGITAL CUSTOMIZATION

Digital textile pattern by Eye Dazzler Textile Design Studio

HANNAH ROSS is a fashion designer and textile artist. She interned for Eye Dazzler in autumn 2012.

What skills will a young designer need if they want to work with a digital print house? To work at a digital print house you will need to be able to draw, paint, collage, spray paint, etc. Since multiple prints are created each day, you must be able to work quickly on the computer, often using one design inspiration to create four or five different prints. Don't over think, just do!

What skills do you think this internship added to your capabilities as a fashion designer? I furthered my textile knowledge and computer design skills. I now have an understanding of the dynamics of an independent design company. One day, I would love to operate an independent design house where a team of close, passionate people is working together to create beauty. After interning at Eye Dazzler, I realized it is as important to foster an environment of personal relationship as one of creative responsibility. In a small environment, negative feelings will kill the creative juices.

Using knowledge gained at Eye Dazzler, what advice can you give an emerging designer looking to customize his or her own textiles through digital print? First, what dyes are being used? Fibre reactive is less environmentally harmful but not as bright; acids are toxic but you get much brighter colours. Small details will not read very well. If the print is fewer than five colours, you may want to consider silkscreen for a sharper image and cleaner colours. Digital printing does not penetrate the fabric and works best on thin, natural fibre wovens. Stretch fabrics will lose image quality when worn.

APPENDIX

TRADE SHOW CALENDAR

LINKS

m+a international, Exhibition Database by Country – www.expodatabase.com
Modem Online, Professional Art & Design Information – www.modemonline.com

TRADE SHOW	FOCUS	LOCATION	DATE
Printsource	Textile & Surface Design	New York, USA	Jan/Apr/Jul
Première Vision Pluriel		Paris, France	Feb/Sept
Expofil	Yarns & Fibres		
Première Vision	Textiles		
Le Cuir à Paris	Fur & Leather		
Indigo Paris	Surface Design		
ModAmont	Trims/Hardware		
Zoom	European Fashion Manufacturing		
Première Vision NY	Textile	New York, NY	Jan/Jul
Indigo by Première Vision	Textile & Surface Design	New York, USA	Jan/April/Jul
		Brussels, Germany	Feb/Sept
Denim by Première Vision	Denim	Paris, France	Nov/May
		Shanghai, China	March
Texworld	Textiles	Paris, France	Feb/Sept
Accessorie Circuit/ENK	Accessories	New York, USA	Jan/May/Aug
Coterie/ENK	Womens Contemporary & RTW	New York, USA	Feb/Sept
Moda Manhattan	Ready To Wear	New York, USA	Feb/May/Aug/Sept
Designers & Agents	Womans Contemporary	New York, USA	Jan/Feb/May/Sept
		Los Angeles, USA	Jan/Mar/Jun/Oct
		Paris, France	Mar/Sept
MAN	Mens	Paris, France	Jan
		New York, USA	Jan
Fame	Juniors Contemporary	New York, USA	Feb/May/Aug/Sept
Pitti Uomo	Mens	Florence, Italy	Jan/June
Pitti W	Womans	Florence, Italy	Jan/June
Ethical Fashion Show Berlin	Eco-Streetwear/Casual Wear	Berlin, Germany	Jan
Who's Next	Première Fashion & Accessories	Paris, France	July
Scoop	Boutique Womenswear	London, UK	Feb
WWD Magic	Apparel/Accessories/Shoes	Las Vegas, USA	Feb/Aug
Capsule	Premium Streetwear, Independent and Contemporary	Berlin, Germany	Jan/Jul
		Las Vegas, USA	Feb/Aug
	Mens	Paris, France	Jan/Jul
		New York, USA	Jan/Jul
	Womens	New York, USA	Feb/Sept
		Paris, France	Mar/Sept
Première Classe	Accessories	Paris, France	March

SOURCING AND SELECTING
TEXTILES FOR FASHION

CHAPTER ONE: THE ROLE OF TEXTILES IN FASHION
CHAPTER TWO: MATERIALS
CHAPTER THREE: SURFACE DESIGN
CHAPTER FOUR: CONCEPTUALIZING THE COLLECTION
CHAPTER FIVE: SOURCING YOUR TEXTILE
CHAPTER SIX: TEXTILE AND THE COLLECTION
SOURCING INTERVIEWS
APPENDIX

200

GLOSSARY

A

Accreditation bodies — governmental or private sector associations of international scope that develop evaluation standards and criteria for business and products

Acetate — a synthetic textile made from cellulosic acetate

Acid wash — wash process that produces a frosted effect on dyed fabrics

Appliqué — method of sewing shaped scraps of fabric onto a textile ground to create pattern and texture

Automated screen-printing — mechanized form of screen printing (see screen printing)

Avant garde — French language term used to refer to experimental or innovative work in the arts fields

B

Baroque — stylistic movement of the seventeenth century emphasizing bold curves, elaborate symmetry and dramatic ornamentation

Batik — a dye resist technique that uses wax to prevent absorption of dye stuff by the textile

Batting — non woven material often of polyester, cotton or wool that gives loft to textile projects

Beading — method of stitching beads in decorative patterns onto the surface of a textile

Bias cut — technique of cutting a woven textile on an angle to the weft and warp threads to increase stretch

Bit map — (also known as raster); computerized language based on a grid of coloured pixels, best for photographic representation

Blended yarn — yarn containing two or more fibre types

Block print — A) traditional method of printing by hand using carved wooden blocks B) resulting printed pattern

Boning — technique of stiffening a garment with stays traditionally made of whale bone

Braid — a decorative trim of repetitively interwoven strands of three or more

C

CAD (computer aided design) — the use of various computer programs to aid in the design of a product

Camouflage — modern stylized and abstracted landscape motifs used originally in combat uniforms

Cellulose fibre — a filament produced from the seedpod, stalk, or leaf of a plant

Chinoiserie — textile patterns that incorporate Asian motifs

Chintz — woven and glazed cotton fabric printed with brightly coloured floral patterns; originally from India

Construction — A) re: textile, any method of intertwining threads or yarns to form a textile B) re garment: method of various sewing techniques to create a three-dimensional garment

Conversational — pattern created from repetitive pictorial representations of everyday items

Converter — intermediary who buys up large amounts of raw textiles called greige goods and has the fabrics dyed, printed or otherwise finished and then sells to the consumer

Collection — a selection of garments or looks put out by a fashion brand for a given season

Colour fast — dye colour that will not run or fade with wash and wear

Colour story — a selected palette or grouping of colours

Copper plate printing — form of intaglio printing developed in 1752 by Francis Dixon allowing for highly detailed patterns to be printed on textiles

Copyright — legal rights granted to the producer or distributor of a work of art guaranteeing exclusive ownership and usage

Cotton gin — machine invented by Eli Whitney that separates cotton fibres from the hull and seeds

Croquis — template of various standardized human forms utilized when creating fashion sketches or technical flats

Crystal dye — dye technique that leaves a shattered glass pattern on the textile

D

Damask — a sturdy textile of rich patterns formed by satin weave threads on a plain weave ground, usually made from silk, linen or cotton

Dip dye — dye technique where cloth is dipped into the dye bath to create colour variation effects

Ditsy — miniaturized scattered pattern of any motif

DPI (dots per inch) — the standard of measurement for quality in digital print, refers directly to the amount of ink droplets that are found in a square inch of print

Drape — textile property referring to the fabric's ability to fall gracefully in space

Draping — the manipulation of textile on a dress form or human body to create fashion apparel

Dye bath — a solution in which dye is dissolved

Dye book — a promotional booklet offered by a dye works showcasing swatches of textiles in the dye colours offered

Dye sublimation — Printing process in which dyes are transferred to a receiver sheet by a digitally driven thermal printhead; variations in temperature control the amount of dye that sublimates, thus varying the colour intensity; dye can then be heat transferred from sheet to printable surface

E

Element — one image used for a pattern repeat

Embellishment — the addition of decorative three-dimensional objects to the design of a textile surface

Enzyme wash — special wash process to give fabrics a worn-in look and feel, used especially with denim

201

TRADE SHOW CALENDAR
GLOSSARY
RESOURCES FOR TEXTILES AND SUPPLIES
INDEX
IMAGE CREDITS
ACKNOWLEDGEMENTS

F

Fabric manipulation — art of reshaping the surface of a textile through various techniques, both structural and decorative

Face — the right side of a textile

Fashion calendar — fashion industry schedule of shows and collection releases based on the seasonal calendar

Fashion figure — elongated and stylized human form used in fashion illustration

Felt — A) act of creating a textile by matting fibres using heat and water B) textile created from this process

Filament yarn — any yarn created from one (monofilament) or multiple (multifilament) continuous strands of fibre

Finishing — any manufacturing process that enhances the qualities of a textile after the construction process

Flatbed screen-printing — machines that use a series of screens with automated squeegees to print multicolour images

Float — section of yarn pulled out of a woven textile that travels across the back of the textile before being reintroduced to create patterns

Forecasting — the act of interpreting future trends by analysing information from today

Free embroidery — embroidery style in which the designs and stitches are not based on the weave of the underlying fabric

Fringe — A decorative border or edging of hanging threads, cords, or strips, often attached to a separate band

G

Gather — sewing technique of piling soft folds of fabric along a loose stitch to create fullness in a garment

Geometric print — any print or pattern utilizing geometric shapes in repeat or abstraction

Gesture — drawing style that captures the overall expression of the subject to emphasize an idea, sentiment, or attitude

Grain — the directional pattern created by warp (lengthwise) and weft (crosswise) threads in a woven textile

Greige goods — any textile that has not been dyed or printed

Grommet — ring of metal or plastic that can be inserted into a textile to create a permanent hole

H

Handicraft — A) occupation requiring skilled hand work B) an object fashioned from such work

High-low fashion collaborations — any fashion project presented by a partnership of a well-known designer and mass market retailer

Hue — the quality of a colour in its purest form

I

Ikat — traditional weaving technique in which the warp threads are space dyed previously to allow a pattern to emerge when woven

J

Jacquard loom — programmable loom that simplifies the manufacturing of complex patterned weaves such as brocade, damask and matelasse

Jobber — intermediary that buys fabrics from mills, converters, importers and designers and sells to the consumer

K

Kevlar — first textile with engineered fire- and abrasion-resistant properties

Knit — A) the act of interlocking yarns into rows of repetitive loops that create chains of stitches B) the resultant textile

Knitting machine — any machine that produces a knit textile

L

Linen —A) a natural fibre produced by the flax plant B) a cloth woven from the yarns produced by this fibre

Loom — a device that allows threads to be interlaced at right angles to form a textile

Low water immersion — dye process that uses a low water-to-textile ratio

M

Machine embroidery — modern mechanized method of embroidering textiles capable of mimicking almost all hand techniques

Market segmentation — classifying a brand's market level on the common needs and spending patterns of perspective buyers

Merchandise segmentation — categorizing merchandise by the section of population most likely to buy it

Metal spikes — surface design trim element that come in various metal finishes and pointed silhouettes

Microfibre — miniaturized synthetic fibres that measure less then one denier in length

Mineral wash — a specialized textile wash process that can create various dye and fade pattern variations on the textile's surface

Mini-crinis — a short hoop skirt introduced by Vivienne Westwood in the mid-1980s

Mordant dye — a dyestuff that becomes fixed to a textile through the addition of a reagent such as tannic acid

Muslin — A) inexpensive woven cotton textiles of various weights B) prototype of fashion garment made in this fabric

N

Nailheads — surface trim that resembles the head of a nail, often used on leather and accessory fashion items

Nylon — first commercially successful man-made textile derived from synthetic polymers

O

Ombre — method of dyeing a textile by slowly adding the textile into the dye bath to create a gradation of colour or value

Op art — abstract art characterized by bold geometric shapes and contrasting colour palettes that create optical illusions

SOURCING AND SELECTING
TEXTILES FOR FASHION

CHAPTER ONE: THE ROLE OF TEXTILES IN FASHION
CHAPTER TWO: MATERIALS
CHAPTER THREE: SURFACE DESIGN
CHAPTER FOUR: CONCEPTUALIZING THE COLLECTION
CHAPTER FIVE: SOURCING YOUR TEXTILE
CHAPTER SIX: TEXTILE AND THE COLLECTION
SOURCING INTERVIEWS
APPENDIX

202

Open-end spinning — a process for turning fibres into yarns at high speeds without using a spindle, resulting yarns are course and have an uneven directional lay

Over dying — technique of applying dye over a previously dyed or printed textile

Over run — goods that have been produced surplus to orders

P

Paisley — pattern created from stylized florals and swirling raindrop shapes

Patchwork — sewing technique of stitching multiple scraps of fabric to create one textile

Pattern block — the smallest section of non-repetitive imagery in a pattern

Persist — water-based product used to resist dye from being absorbed by a textile

Pigment dye — class of dye that sits on top of the textile fibre and fades over time leaving a very soft hand and worn-in look

Plaids — pattern formed by intersecting stripes based on the 90-degree angles of warp and weft

Ply yarn — yarn produced by twisting together two or more yarn strands

Polka dot — repetitive use of circles to create pattern

Polyester — A) a petroleum-based synthetic fibre with high abrasion resistance and low absorbency B) any woven or knit textile made from this fibre

Potato dextrin — a potato-based starch dye resist that leaves a cracked and lacey effect on fabric

Primary colour — set of three colours that can be combined to create a useful spectrum of colours

Principles of design — concepts used to organize the structural elements of design: rhythm, movement/emphasis, gradation, repetition, contrast, balance, unity and proportion

Protein fibre — a filament gathered from the fur of an animal with the exception of silk

Psychedelic — modern abstract patterns originating in the 1960s marked by bright acid colours and outlandish motifs

Pyramid studs — surface trim that resembles a small metal pyramid

Q

Quilting — sewing technique that uses stitching to decoratively catch a three-dimensional filler between two sheets of fabric

R

Rayon — A) Any of several synthetic textile fiberes produced by forcing a cellulose solution through fine spinnerets and solidifying the resulting filaments B) A fabric so woven or knit

Reactive dye — class of colourfast dye that forms a chemical bond with hydroxyl groups in the textile fibres

Regenerated fibre — a filament manufactured by dissolving a plant- or animal-based material and regenerating the material through extrusion and precipitation

Registered identification number (RIN) — number issued by the Federal Trade Commission in the US to a business engaged in the manufacture, import, export or distribution of textile, wool or fur products

Rice paste — paste created from powdered rice that can be applied to a textile to resist cool water dye bath absorption

Ring spinning — process of yarn production that both twists and draws that yarn around a ring, simultaneously winding it onto a bobbin

Rococo — art movement of the early 18th century that started in France, marked by elaborate asymmetrical and organic ornamentation and a relaxed attitude

Roller printing — mechanized form of textile printing that uses a series of engraved cylinders to transfer ink onto fabric

Rotary screen-printing — printing machine that forces ink through a perforated cylinder onto fabric to apply an image

Ruffle — a strip of gathered or pleated fabric used for trim or decoration

S

Screen-printing — process of using a squeegee to force ink through a partially blocked fabric screen onto a surface material

Seamless repeat — an element of a pattern that flows without separation or distinction once put into a repetitive pattern

Secondary colours — coloured derived from mixing two primary colours in a given colour space

Selvedge — tightly interlaced length wise edge of a woven textile

Shibori — A) an ancient Japanese dye technique which uses threads stitched or wrapped to hold back dye stuff from textile absorption B) same methods used with the application of steam or heat to form permanent shapes in a textile

Silk — A) long fibrous thread produced by the silk worm B) woven textile produced from this thread

Smocking — sewing technique that controls fullness in a garment by shirring together small vertical rows of gathers

Snap — garment closure that fastens shut by attaching male and female components

Sodium alginate — a colourless crystalline compound used as a thickener in food or dyes

Space dye — a technique of adding different coloured dyes to sections of a yarn or thread

Spandex — A) elastic synthetic textile fibre made mainly from polyurethane B) thread or textile made from this fibre

Splatter — dye effect in which dye is dripped or thrown onto the surface of a textile or garment

Spinning Jenny — an early spinning machine employing several spindles

Spray method — dye technique where the dye is projected from a spray bottle or air brush onto the surface of a textile or garment

Spot (nearby) goods — textile goods that are still in production but close to being done

Spun yarn — yarn created from staple fibres spun together to create a continuous strand

Staple fibre — any non continuous fibre (generally natural) that can be twisted with other short fibres to create a continuous strand

Stone wash — a wash process using pumice stones or chemicals to achieve an uneven faded effect on textiles

Surface design — any decorative design element added to the surface of a textile or garment

Synthetic fabrics — textile of any construction method created from any man-made fibre

Synthetic fibre — any filament produced exclusively from petrochemicals in a chemical process

T

Target market — a select group of consumers, defined by various lifestyle and spending patterns, deemed most likely to buy from a brand

Tariffs — taxes collected by a government on the value of an imported product including freight and insurance

Tassel — a bell-shaped trim made from a cluster of string, ropes or chain folded in half and gathered at the neck

Textile properties — aspects and characteristics of a textile such as abrasion resistance (functional) or texture (aesthetic)

Tie-dye — modern method of folding and binding textiles prior to dyeing to create colour patterns

Toile — A) printed textile pattern in one colour on light background depicting pastoral scenes B) prototype of a garment made in inexpensive fabric to test design and fit C) inexpensive woven textile generally cotton or linen

Trade laws — the rules and customs for handling trade between countries

Trademark — law protecting a product that has been officially registered and legally restricted to the use of the owner or manufacturer

Tribal (folk) — textiles that mimic traditional art styles and fabric patterns from around the globe

Trickle-down effect — the fashion theory based on fashion trends flowing from the upper level of societies to the general public

Trickle-up effect — fashion theory based on fashion trends flowing from the streets to well-known fashion designers or mavens

Trim — a decoration or adornment

Tucks — narrow folds or pleats of fabric secured fully or partially along their length by stitching

U

Upcycling — off-shoot of sustainability in fashion in which a designer will create new textiles or garments from an already manufactured and used or worn textile.

V

Vat dyes — form of chemically produced dyes that are water insoluble and extremely light- and wash-fast

Vector — computer graphics language based on x and y axis, capable of mathematically proportionate reduction and enlargement without loss of detail

Vertical pleat — sewing technique that presses sharp folds into the vertical line of a garment, increasing fullness

Vertically integrated mill — mill that sources fibres, manufactures yarns, and constructs and finishes the fabrics

Vinyl — category of flexible, shiny plastics with textile-like properties used in the manufacturing of apparel and accessories

Viscose — a synthetic textile made from viscous solution of cellulose xanthate

W

Wacom tablet — trademark for a computerized drawing tablet that allows for direct transfer of hand drawing into a computer program

Warp — threads or yarns set lengthwise on a loom or in a woven textile

Weft — threads or yarns that fill horizontally on a loom or in a woven textile

Wool — A) dense hair of sheep, goats and some other hoofed animals that can be shorn and spun to produce a natural yarn B) textile produced by these yarns

Woven textile — any fabric created from the under and over repetitive intertwining of weft (horizontal running) and warp (vertical running) threads, can be produced by hand or on a loom

Y

Yarn — a continuous strand formed by twisting together threads of various man-made or synthetic fibres, to be used in knitting or weaving

Z

Zeitgeist — the stylistic movement or intellectual school of thought that defines and influences the culture of a given era; the spirit of the times

SOURCING AND SELECTING
TEXTILES FOR FASHION

CHAPTER ONE: THE ROLE OF TEXTILES IN FASHION
CHAPTER TWO: MATERIALS
CHAPTER THREE: SURFACE DESIGN
CHAPTER FOUR: CONCEPTUALIZING THE COLLECTION
CHAPTER FIVE: SOURCING YOUR TEXTILE
CHAPTER SIX: TEXTILE AND THE COLLECTION
SOURCING INTERVIEWS
APPENDIX

204

RESOURCES FOR TEXTILES AND SUPPLIES

USA – EAST

Aljo Dyes
54 2nd Avenue
Brooklyn, NY 11215
(718) 788-3930
www.aljodye.com/main.html
Acid, basic, disperse, direct, fibre,
reactive and vat dyes

B&J Fabrics
525 7th Ave
New York, NY 10018
(212)354-8150
www.bandjfabrics.com
Variety of both wovens and knits

Botani
263 W. 36th Street,
NY, New York 11018
(212)244-3222
www.botanitrim.com
handbag hardware, buttons and ribbons

Craig's Prints
247 West 38th St. Suite 606
New York, NY 10018
(212)947-1593
www.craigsprints.com
Custom digital fabric printing

Daytona Trimmings Company
251 W 39th St
New York, NY 10018
(212) 354-1713
Trims with a focus on lace and ribbons

Eye Dazzler Studio
174 Bogart St. #204
Brooklyn, NY 11206
(917) 517-3853
www.eyedazzlerdesign.com
In-house and custom digital textile design

Galbraith & Paul
116 Shur Lane
Philadelphia, PA 19127
(215)508-0800
www.galbraithandpaul.com
Hand block printed textiles

Gowanus Print Lab
54 2nd Avenue
Brooklyn, NY 11215
(718) 788-3930
www.gowanusprintlab.com
DIY screen printing lab, gallery, lesson,
studio space rental, and supplies

Leather Impact
256 West 38th St.
New York, NY 10018
(212) 301-2332
www.leatherimpact.com
Whole skins, partials , trims and tools

M&J Trimming
1008 Sixth Avenue
New York, NY 10018
(212)391-6200
www.mjtrim.com
Trims, beads, crystals, closures, cords,
tassels, supplies and notions

Metro Custom Dyeing
306 W. 38th St.
Ny, New York 10018
(212)391-1001
www.metrodyeing.com
Machine dyeing, garment dyeing, custom
dye patterns

Mood Fabrics
225 West 37th St #3
New York, NY 10018
(212)730-5003
www.moodfabrics.com
Wide variety offabrics, notions, trims

New York Embroidery Studio
327 W 36th St, 111 Floor
NY, New York 10018
(212)971-9102
www.nyembroiderystudio.com
Embroidery, beading, cutting, pleating,
heat transfer, embellishments

Pacific Trimming
218 West 38th Street New York, NY 10018
(212) 279-9310
Zippers, buttons, snaps, grommets
and trims. Custom setting of metal
components and sizing of zippers

Paron West & Paron Annex
206 West 40th St
New York, NY 10018
(212) 768-3266
www.paronfabrics.com
Two stores of designer fabrics, one full
price, the other discount

Pearl Trim & Textile
721 West Grange Ave
Philadelphia, PA 19120
(877)424-9030
Fabrics, trims, bias bindings, speciality
items

Standard Screen
121 Varick Street
New York, NY 10013
(212) 627-2727
www.standardscreen.com
screen printing supplies, screen burning
services

Victory Factory
18410 Jamaica Avenue
Queens, NY 11423
(718) 454-2255
www.victoryfactory.com
Screen printing supplies, screen burning
services

USA – WEST

Beads and More
800 Maple Avenue
Los Angeles, CA 90014
(213) 955-9000

LA Alex Inc
418 E 9th St.
Los Angeles, CA 90079
(213)489-3010
Great prices, large selection of fabrics,
notions and trims

Los Angeles Dye & Wash Co
6849 E. Washington Blvd
Commerce, CA 90040
(323) 724-7878
www.losangelesdye.com/
All dye and wash techniques, custom
colour

LA Gentex Corporation
529 Stanford Ave.
Los Angeles, CA 90013
(213) 623-7709
www.lagentex.com/
Garment dyeing for all size businesses

Mendel's Far Out Fabrics
1556 Haight Street
San Francisco, CA 94117
(415) 621-1287
www.mendels.com/creativity2.shtml
Basic sewing notions, trims, beads,
crystals, feathers, art supplies

Mike's Fabrics
821 Wall St.
Los Angeles, CA 90014
(213)624-3038
Large selection of fabrics

My Long Sewing Machines, Fabrics and Trims
11662 Trask Ave
Garden Grove, CA 92843
714-537-2408

Target Trim Co.
629 East 9th Street
Los Angeles, CA 90015
(213) 489-4449
www.targettrim.com
Large selection of trims, lace, notions

INTERNATIONAL/INTERNET

Aurora
Specialty Textiles Group, Inc
www.auroratextile.com
Multi-functional textile finishing
USA

Hussein Fabrics
52A High St.
Walthamstow, London, UK
E17 7LD
+44(0)20 8520 7676
Top quality discounted fabrics**
** Walthamstow is full of small end roll fabric shops

MacCulloch and Wallis
25-26 Dering St
London, Greater London, UK
W1S 1AT
+44(0)20 7629 0311
www.macculloch-wallis.co.uk
Fabrics trims and supplies

Marché Saint Pierre
2 Rue Charles Nodier
75018 Paris, France
+33 1 46 06 92 25
www.marchesaintpierre.com
Five floors of amazing slection

Spoon Flower
www.spoonflower.com
Customized digital print fabrics
USA

The African Fabric Shop
19 Hebble Mount
Meltham, Holmfirth
West Yorkshire
HD9 4HG
UK (by appointment only)
www.africanfabric.co.uk
Hand woven traditional fabrics

Top Fabric of SoHo
www.topfabric.co.uk
+44(0)20 7494 1666
Large variety of top quality fabrics
UK

BUSINESS

British Fashion Council
U5 Portland Place
London, UK
W1B 1PW
+44(0)20 7636 7788
www.britishfashioncouncil.co.uk

Council of Fashion Designers of America
USA
www.cfda.com
info@cfda.com

Gov.UK
www.gov.uk/browse/business

SCORE
USA
www.score.org
help@score.org
800-634-0245
Many office locations, free business mentoring

Small Business Administration
USA
www.sba.gov
800-827-5722
US Small Business Administration
409 3rd st, SW
Washington, DC 20416
Many office locations, business advice and help

Small Business UK
www.smallbusiness.co.uk
Online only, no individual counselling

Start Up Fashion
USA
www.startupfashion.com
hello@startupfashion.com
StartUP FASHION LLC
PO 1611
New York, NY 10013
Fashion-specific business advice and help

GREEN

Centre for Sustainable Fashion
UK
www.sustainable-fashion.com

Dharma Trading Co.
1604 Fourth St.
San Rafeal, CA 94901
800-524-5227
www.dharmatrading.com
Many green textiles and finishing products

Eco Fashion Week
USA
www.ecofashion-week.com

EcoTextile News
UK
+44(0) 1977 708488
www.ecotextile.com
For news and information on green fabrics

Green Business Network
UK
+44(0) 01924 405028
www.greenbusinessnetwork.org.uk
Sustainable business advice

Noon Design Studio
407 E Pico Blvd, suite 1000
Los Angeles, CA 90015
(773) 844-1163
www.noondesignstudio.com
Natural dye production house

Organic Cotton Plus
(855) SEW-PURE
www.organiccottonplus.com
Variety of eco textiles and supplies

Sew Eco-Logical
1280-B East 28th Ave
Eugene OR 97403
(541) 683-6333
www.seworganic.com
Open stock certified organic textiles

Source4Style
500 7th Ave, FLR 17
New York, NY 10019
info@source4style.com
www.source4style.com
Connects designers with global textile suppliers

Sustainable Business
USA
(631) 423-3277
www.sustainablebusiness.com

SOURCING AND SELECTING
TEXTILES FOR FASHION

CHAPTER ONE: THE ROLE OF TEXTILES IN FASHION
CHAPTER TWO: MATERIALS
CHAPTER THREE: SURFACE DESIGN
CHAPTER FOUR: CONCEPTUALIZING THE COLLECTION
CHAPTER FIVE: SOURCING YOUR TEXTILE
CHAPTER SIX: TEXTILE AND THE COLLECTION
SOURCING INTERVIEWS
APPENDIX

206

INDEX

207

TRADE SHOW CALENDAR
GLOSSARY
RESOURCES FOR TEXTILES AND SUPPLIES
INDEX
IMAGE CREDITS
ACKNOWLEDGEMENTS

Compiled by
Indexing Specialists (UK) Ltd.,
Indexing House,
306A Portland Road, Hove,
East Sussex BN3 5LP
United Kingdom.
+44(0)1273 416777.
indexers@indexing.co.uk
www.indexing.co.uk

IMAGE CREDITS

ACKNOWLEDGEMENTS

I would like to thank the following people for their influence and contributions: Katherine Ellis for teaching me to sew; Lynn Johnstone Leonard for getting my art career underway; Lorraine Orenchuk for fostering my writing and Renee Levin for the opportunity to be her head designer. • In addition I would like to thank Leafy Cummins for the opportunity to write this book. Her advice, patience and support through the process were invaluable. Rachel Parkinson and Renee Villanueva Last did an amazing job organizing a completely unorganized image list. Regan Loggans for her research efforts during the first chapters of this book. Thank you to everyone who contributed interviews and images; your participation has enhanced the book tremendously. • I would like to thank my family. My husband Martin and daughter Rose for their love and support. • This book is dedicated to my parents, Dennis and Peggy, who always encouraged me to be myself and follow my dreams even when it appeared I had no idea what I was doing. • The publisher would like to thank the following for their reviews of the manuscript: Bo Breda, Amanda Briggs-Goode, Deirdre Campion, Jason Paul McCarthy, Brigitte Stockton, Frances Turner.